PROSE

SHORT
FORMS

BRIAN KELLOW • JOHN KRISAK

Prentice-Hall Canada Inc.
Scarborough, Ontario

Canadian Cataloguing in Publication Data

Main entry under title:
Prose : short forms
ISBN 0-13-715301-5

1. Literature—Collections. 2. Prose literature.
3. Readers (Secondary). I. Kellow, Brian. II. Krisak, John.
PN6014.P76 1990   808.88'8   C90-093777-7

Prentice-Hall, Inc., Englewood Cliffs, New Jersey
Prentice-Hall International, Inc., London
Prentice-Hall of Australia, Pty., Ltd., Sydney
Prentice-Hall of India Pvt., Ltd., New Delhi
Prentice-Hall of Japan, Inc., Tokyo
Prentice-Hall of Southeast Asia (PTE) Ltd., Singapore
Editora Prentice-Hall do Brasil Ltda., Rio de Janeiro
Prentice-Hall Hispanoamericana, S.A., Mexico

1 2 3 4 5 6 JDC 95 94 93 92 91 90

Printed and bound in Canada by John Deyell Company

Acquiring Editor: *David Steele*
Program Manager: *Alan Simpson*
Project Editor: *MaryBeth Leatherdale, Jennifer Taylor*
Production Editor: *Evelyn Maksimovich*
Manufacturing: *Crystale Chalmers*
Design: *Anita Macklin*
Typesetter: *Q Composition Inc.*
Cover: *Emily Carr*
         Old Time Coast Village
         91.5 × 128.3 cm.
         Collection of the Vancouver Art Gallery
         Emily Carr Trust, 1942

Policy Statement
Prentice-Hall Canada Inc., School Division, and the editors of *Prose: Short Forms*
are committed to the publication of instructional materials that are as bias-free
as possible. This anthology was evaluated for bias prior to publication.
   The editors and publisher also recognize the importance of appropriate reading
levels and have therefore made every effort to ensure the highest degree of
readability in the student text. The content has been selected, organized, and
written at a level suitable to the intended audience.

Table of Contents

Unit One   Learning to Learn

Unit Two   Values and Choices

Unit Five Aging

Unit Six Loving

Unit Seven **The Earth and Us**

ACKNOWLEDGEMENTS

This project has been enriched by the support of many people—colleagues, friends and family whose help we would now like to formally acknowledge. Special thanks are also extended to the following people at Prentice-Hall Canada Inc. whose contributions to this book have been extensive and with whom we have worked so closely—David Steele, MaryBeth Leatherdale, Evelyn Maksimovich, Crystale Chalmers and Anita Macklin.

John Krisak
Brian Kellow

For Paulette and Margaret.

Learning
to
Learn

The Credo

Robert Fulghum

> List the things you have learned in school which are helpful to you in living your life. Compare your list with the lists of other members of your class.

Each spring, for many years, I have set myself the task of writing a personal statement of belief: a Credo. When I was younger, the statement ran for many pages, trying to cover every base, with no loose ends. It sounded like a Supreme Court brief, as if words could resolve all conflicts about the meaning of existence.

The Credo has grown shorter in recent years—sometimes cynical, sometimes comical, sometimes bland—but I keep working at it. Recently I set out to get the statement of personal belief down to one page in simple terms, fully understanding the naive idealism that implied.

The inspiration for brevity came to me at a gasoline station. I managed to fill an old car's tank with super-deluxe high-octane go-juice. My old hoopy couldn't handle it and got the willies—kept sputtering out at intersections and belching going downhill. I understood. My mind and my spirit get like that from time to time. Too much high-content information, and *I* get the existential willies—keep sputtering out at intersections where life choices must be made and I either know too much or not enough. The examined life is no picnic.

I realized then that I already know most of what's necessary to live a meaningful life—that it isn't all that complicated. *I know it.* And have known it for a long, long time. Living it—well, that's another matter, yes? Here's my Credo:

All I really need to know about how to live and what to do and how to be I learned in kindergarten. Wisdom was not at the top of the graduate-school mountain, but there in the sandpile at Sunday School. These are the things I learned:

Share everything.
Play fair.
Don't hit people.
Put things back where you found them.
Clean up your own mess.
Don't take things that aren't yours.
Say you're sorry when you hurt somebody.
Wash your hands before you eat.
Flush.
Warm cookies and cold milk are good for you.
Live a balanced life—learn some and think some and draw and
  paint and sing and dance and play and work every day some.
Take a nap every afternoon.
When you go out into the world, watch out for traffic, hold hands,
  and stick together.
Be aware of wonder. Remember the little seed in the Styrofoam cup:
  The roots go down and the plant goes up and nobody really
  knows how or why, but we are all like that.
Goldfish and hamsters and white mice and even the little seed in
  the Styrofoam cup—they all die. So do we.
And then remember the Dick-and-Jane books and the first word you
  learned—the biggest word of all—LOOK.

Everything you need to know is in there somewhere. The Golden Rule and love and basic sanitation. Ecology and politics and equality and sane living.

Take any one of those items and extrapolate it into sophisticated adult terms and apply it to your family life or your work or your government or your world and it holds true and clear and firm. Think what a better world it would be if we all—the whole world— had cookies and milk about three o'clock every afternoon and then lay down with our blankies for a nap. Or if all governments had as a basic policy to always put things back where they found them and to clean up their own mess.

And it is still true, no matter how old you are—when you go out into the world, it is best to hold hands and stick together.

RESPONSE

1. What does Fulghum's list of what he learned in school have in common with yours?

2. Fulghum asserts that his credo contains "everything you need to know." Explain why you agree or disagree with him.

EXTENSION

3. Select a statement from Fulghum's credo. Recount an incident from your own life that illustrates the value of Fulghum's advice.

4. Compose your own credo. You might want to record it in your journal.

Eliciting Human Potential

Sydney J. Harris

What do you want your education to do for you?

What are the differences between teaching and coaching?

Speaking at a commencement of graduating teachers, I said that my whole message could be summed up in fewer than fifty words uttered by Goethe nearly two centuries ago: "If you treat a person as he is, he will stay as he is; but if you treat him as if he were what he ought to be and could be, he will become what he ought to be and could be."

This applies to most pupils everywhere; and the best teacher is not one who crams the most *into* a pupil, but who gets the most *out* of one. Education is a process not of stuffing people, like sausage into a casing, but of eliciting from people the potentialities hidden even from themselves.

And Goethe's sage comment applies to far more than teachers and pupils. I am constantly surprised at how many parents stereotype their own children at a certain age and persist in regarding them in the same light year after year, so that the child loses its motivation and incentive to change.

Actually, children themselves do the same with their peers. Once a child receives a certain reputation among his classmates, their conditioned responses almost force him to maintain the same role, and it is devilishly difficult, if not impossible, to reverse the early image.

This is why, by the way, so many children in the later grades want to change schools and cannot give their parents any "sensible" reason. They are ashamed to admit or only half-conscious of the fact that they would like to break out of the mold in which they were cast at an early age and seek a new personal identity for themselves.

In marriage as well, the mates often regard and treat one another only as the persons they were when first wed, so that efforts to develop and grow and change are met with puzzlement, scorn, or resentment. We feel most comfortable, even with those we presumably care for, when we can put people into pigeonholes and keep them there.

There is something valuable to be learned here from a good coach or trainer, who regards his charge not as the person he is but as if he were about to become the person he ought to be and could be, in Goethe's words. The coach works with the potentialities, not only with the actualities, and recognizes that the desire to develop and improve is as vital a part of the person as his physical or mental makeup.

But this capacity, except in unusual cases, is as easily discouraged as encouraged; people sink back into themselves when they perceive that their teachers, their parents, or their mates persist in ignoring or rejecting an effort to shed the old skin and become what William James called twice-born.

Most people, I am convinced, have a residual capacity to rise to the level of expectations, to meet standards and goals, and to become more than they were. Only the most aggressive and determined can accomplish this against odds; the rest need help, but they usually find that more people than pigeons are put in pigeonholes.

RESPONSE

1. In your experience, is Goethe's statement true?

2. According to Harris, what factors prevent people from developing their full potential? Explain why you agree or disagree with Harris.

EXTENSION

3. In small groups, compile a list of common expressions which "pigeonhole" people; for example, "He or she is the kind of person who. . . ." Write an editorial on the injustice of one of these expressions.

4. Write a journal entry about being pigeonholed by a teacher or family member. Be sure to include a description of your feelings at the time and how you feel now about the incident.

Ultimate Discourse

E. L. Doctorow

> In small groups, recount the story you most frequently tell about yourself.
>
> Write a journal entry reflecting upon why you tell this story about yourself.

When I was a boy everyone in my family was a good story-teller, my mother and father, my brother, my aunts and uncles and grandparents; all of them were people to whom interesting things seemed to happen. The events they spoke of were of a daily, ordinary sort, but when narrated or acted out they took on great importance and excitement as I listened.

Of course, when you bring love to the person you are listening to, the story has to be interesting, and in one sense the task of a professional writer who publishes books is to overcome the terrible loss of not being someone the reader knows and loves.

But apart from that, the people whose stories I heard as a child must have had a very firm view of themselves in the world. They must have been strong enough as presences in their own minds to trust that people would listen to them when they spoke.

I know now that everyone in the world tells stories. Relatively few people are given to mathematics or physics, but narrative seems to be within everyone's grasp, perhaps because it comes of the nature of language itself.

The moment you have nouns and verbs and prepositions, the moment you have subjects and objects, you have stories.

For the longest time there would have been nothing but stories, and no sharper distinction between what was real and what was made up than between what was spoken and what was sung.

Religious arousal and scientific discourse, simple urgent communication and poetry, all burned together in the intense perception of a metaphor—that, for instance, the sun was a god's chariot driven across the heavens.

Stories were as important to survival as a spear or a hoe. They were the memory of the knowledge of the dead. They gave counsel. They connected the visible to the invisible. They distributed the suffering so that it could be borne.

In our era, even as we separate the functions of language, knowing when we speak scientifically we are not speaking poetically, and when we speak theologically we are not speaking the way we do to each other in our houses, and even as our surveys demand statistics, and our courts demand evidence, and our hypotheses demand proof—our minds are still structured for storytelling.

What we call fiction is the ancient way of knowing, the total discourse that antedates all the special vocabularies of modern intelligence.

The professional writer of fiction is a conservative who cherishes the ultimate structures of the human mind. He cultivates within himself the universal disposition to think in terms of conflict and its resolution, and in terms of character undergoing events, and of the outcome of events being not at all sure, and therefore suspenseful—the whole thing done, moreover, from a confidence of narrative that is grounded in our brains as surely as the innate talent to construe the world grammatically.

The fiction writer, looking around him, understands the homage a modern up-to-date world of nonfiction specialists pays to his craft—even as it isolates him and tells him he is a liar. Newsweeklies present the events of the world as installments in a serial melodrama. Weather reports on television are constructed with exact attention to conflict (high-pressure areas clashing with lows), suspense (the climax of tomorrow's prediction coming after the commercial), and the consistency of voice (the personality of the weathercaster). The marketing and advertising of product-facts is unquestionably a fictional enterprise. As is every government's representations of its activities. And modern psychology, with its concepts of *sublimation*, *repression*, *identity crisis*, *complex*, and so on, proposes the interchangeable parts for the stories of all of us; in this sense it is the industrialization of storytelling.

But nothing is as good at fiction as fiction. It is the most ancient way of knowing but also the most modern, managing when it's done right to burn all the functions of language back together into powerful fused revelation. Because it is total discourse it is ultimate discourse. It excludes nothing. It will express from the depth and range of its sources truths that no sermon or experiment or news report can begin to apprehend. It will tell you without shame what people do with their bodies and think with their minds. It will deal evenhandedly with their microbes or their intuitions. It will know their nightmares and blinding moments of moral crisis. You will experience love, if it so chooses, or starvation or drowning or dropping through space or holding a hot pistol in your hand with the police pounding on the door. This is the way it is, it will say, this is what it feels like.

Fiction is democratic, it reasserts the authority of the single mind to make and remake the world. By its independence from all institutions, from the family to the government, and with no responsibility to defend their hypocrisy or murderousness, it is a valuable resource and instrument of survival.

Fiction gives counsel. It connects the present with the past, and the visible with the invisible. It distributes the suffering. It says we must compose ourselves in our stories in order to exist. It says if we don't do it, someone else will do it for us.

RESPONSE

1. What do you think the author means when he says, "Stories were as important to survival as a spear or a hoe"? In what ways do you agree or disagree with him?

2. In your own words, distinguish between *storytelling* and *fiction.*

EXTENSION

3. In the form of fiction, write the story you most frequently tell about yourself.

4. Write a brief essay describing how a work of fiction has influenced you.

Values
and
Choices

Making Hostages of Our Values

Harold Evans

> With a partner or in a small group, devise a definition of *values*. Compile a list of your most important values.

Who said: "The only thing we have to fear is fear itself." "Ask not what your country can do for you; ask what you can do for your country." "Never in the field of human conflict was so much owed by so many to so few"?

The words survive their speakers, and so do their effects. Few of us would challenge the proposition that Franklin Roosevelt, or John Kennedy, or Winston Churchill were well served by the words they chose. World War II may have been the real end of the Depression, but Roosevelt struck the first spark of light for a people who wanted to see a way forward. Kennedy's words raised a surge of idealism in millions of hearts. Churchill's simple sentences stiffened the sinews of England when words were about all they had to use against Hitler.

We like to think we cherish our language. We celebrate our great speeches. We analyze the Gettysburg Address and carve it on our monuments. But while we worship in the cathedrals of rhetoric, we neglect the stones and mortar that build them: The nouns and verbs in everyday use. No one would care to be accused of corrupting the language, but men and women who deal in words sleep soundly at night though all day they have twisted, tortured, beaten and corrupted, diluted and deformed their charges to the confusion and impoverishment of the people.

This has been a week to make us think of our words. Of the hijacked Kuwaiti airliner, Islamic Jihad said: "We declare that we shall execute the Western captives in Lebanon if the plane and the holy warriors aboard are subjected to any military foolhardiness." This meant that a bunch of hijackers would murder their prisoners if force was met with force. The newspaper *USA Today*, among others, fell into the trap. On its front page last Wednesday it reported: "Two Kuwaiti passengers have been executed." This was untrue. Two Kuwaiti passengers were murdered, which is a very different thing. An execution is a punishment for a proved capital offense. It implies a violation of the rule of law; a hearing of evidence; a deliberation; a finding, and a judicial sentencing according to an acknowledged and accepted code of penalties. To use "execution" here is to condemn the innocent, legitimize murder, rationalize terrorism.

This is not an isolated example. It is common. In February, police officer Edward Byrne, a 22-year-old rookie cop, sat in a car in Queens, N.Y., guarding the house of a man who had been threatened because he had reported drug dealing in the district. A car came alongside Byrne's, a man got out, fired five shots through the window of the police car and fled. Newspapers and broadcasters all over the country, including the *New York Times*, referred to this coldblooded murder as an "execution," and the hoodlums as an "execution team." The same corruptions of language were evident when British agents "executed" three IRA members in Gibraltar and when IRA men "executed" two British soldiers at the funeral in Belfast.

The violence that language such as this does to a civilized society can be appreciated by the following sentence: "The state of Louisiana today murdered Leslie Lowenfield, who had been convicted of killing his former girlfriend and four of her relatives."

It is a shocking thought, isn't it, that a state murdered a man? It destroys faith in our institutions. If such an act were reported in reality (instead of being produced by my substitution of the word "murder" for "execution") there would be a public outcry. But it is only as shocking, and as destructive, as the idea that gangsters and terrorists might carry out an "execution."

I am not making a plea simply for avoiding sensationalizing words. As offensive to me—readers may have their own examples—is "child abuse." What does it mean? To abuse is to vilify, revile. This goes nowhere near describing what has been happening. Here is a child locked in an unheated attic whose frostbitten legs had to be amputated at midcalf. Here is a child scalded to death in a welfare "hotel" (another corrupted word).

Here is a child beaten into insensibility. Child abuse may be the legal waffle words, but the reality is cruelty to children. "Cruelty" strikes the imagination in the correct way. "Abuse" anesthetizes the senses.

A society that grows so careless with words makes hostages of all its values.

—U.S. News & World Report, April 25, 1988

RESPONSE

1. a) What does Evans mean when he refers to the "corruption" of words? Explain.
   b) From your own experience, provide two or three examples of the corruption of words.

2. Explain Evans' objections to the use of the terms *execution* and *child abuse*.

3. How is the corruption of language also the corruption of values?

EXTENSION

4. Compose an essay that examines the ways in which external forces threaten one of your values.

5. Choose the value most important to you. Write an account which shows how your everyday behaviour is consistent with this value.

Women's Running

Joan Ullyot

> In an enduring relationship between two people, should one attend to one's own needs before attending to the needs of one's partner?

Back in the early '70s when I first began entering races, reporters would flock around me and the handful of other women runners. In essence, they all wanted to know how we could manage to train for such "grueling" events and still take care of home, husband and kids.

"It's simple," I would respond cheerily. "I just schedule my running first and fit everything else in around it."

Everyone laughed, but I was quite serious. At that point in my running career, training did take precedence over many other activities. That was the major reason I could excel, placing near the top of several national and international championships.

My sons, though only 6 and 8 at the time, supported my efforts. They understood that I was working to get the women's marathon accepted as an Olympic event and wondered if I would train to make the Olympics.

"I'm not sure," I told them. "It would mean concentrated, hard training for a year or more, and TV dinners for you."

The boys gulped but said bravely, "That's OK if it's what you really want, Mom."

I was touched, of course. But by the time the International Olympic Committee recognized the legitimacy of the women's marathon, my boys were away at school and I was a masters runner. I switched my goal to qualifying for the Olympic Trials. Still, it was great to know that the family support was there if I needed it. They gave me permission to be selfish.

The truth is, any athlete hoping to excel has to be somewhat selfish. Runners probably require a little less selfishness than other athletes, since we rarely spend more than 1 or 2 hours a day in training. But the mental effort required to reach peak condition extends far beyond those few hours of actual running.

Here's where women runners are at a great disadvantage compared to men. Given our upbringing and traditions, we struggle to be as selfish as we should. Women are accustomed to being the supportive partner, the homemaker and caretaker. We take pride in our domestic accomplishments.

Sweden's great masters runner Evy Palm bakes her own bread. Joan Samuelson's famous homemade blueberry jam has become a great fund-raiser for the Samantha Smith Foundation.

But what top male runner has cooking, sewing or child-raising as a sideline? It's not expected of men. Running is their career, and they are not criticized for giving it top priority.

Women still are. Grete Waitz, whose husband, Jack, devotes himself to helping her career, has excelled in women's distance running for more than 15 years. Yet reporters frequently ask Grete not about her racing and training, but whether or when she plans to have children. The implication: "Isn't it time to settle down and get on with a woman's *real* business in life?"

Imagine similar questions being asked of Rob de Castella or Toshihiko Seko. It is assumed that their wives will take care of those details.

By and large, top women runners are either single or married to supportive, unselfish husbands. Lisa Martin's husband, Ken, runs at the elite level. He can understand the pressures on Lisa and her need for hard training, so he doesn't feel neglected when she takes the time for two workouts a day.

Priscilla Welch gets coaching as well as encouragement from her husband, David. Ingrid Kristiansen travels with her young son as much as possible, along with a support team of a nanny, coach, masseur and many others.

All these women freely admit that a certain degree of selfishness—of putting their own needs first—is essential to top-level racing. Women whose greatest ambition may be to run a sub-50-minute 10-K or finish a marathon can learn from these examples.

We all have to give ourselves permission to be selfish if we want to achieve our goals. It takes a while to learn this.

When I started running, we were financially stable enough to afford a babysitter to look after the boys while I worked full-time. She stayed late so I could run after work.

This arrangement worked fine except on weekends, when I had no sitter and no chance to run. A typical "good mother," I would skip my training and take the boys to the park.

Finally, I got fed up with this system and decided to whisk the kids off with me to the track. While I ran in circles, they played in the sandy long-jump pit with their matchbox toys.

I still feel guilty that the matchbox toys my children lost in the sand might later have caused ankle sprains to practicing long jumpers. But I have no regrets about adjusting my kids' playtime to conform to my own running schedule.

Even such a small measure of selfishness may be difficult to accept for some women, who feel pressured to put their own needs last. But I think we do our mates and children a favor by letting them fend for themselves now and then.

Some husbands, tiring of frozen dinners or eating out while the wife goes to her weekly running-club workout, may discover a latent talent for cooking. Children can learn to do their own homework. And everyone will be happier with a woman who feels confident enough to train as she must to achieve her goals.

RESPONSE

1. What is your reaction to the author's claim that her family gave her "permission to be selfish"?

2. a) What is the nature of the author's selfishness?
   b) Do you think "selfishness" is the correct term for the author's attitude towards herself? If not, what is the correct term?

3. Explain why you agree or disagree with this statement: "But I think we do our mates and children a favor by letting them fend for themselves now and then."

EXTENSION

4. Write a journal entry describing the last time you did something selfish in the sense meant by Joan Ullyot.

5. Write a composition about the activity in your own life about which you are selfish in the positive sense.

6. Show this article to several people you know and poll their reactions to Joan Ullyot's conception of selfishness.

Fetal Rights

Charlynn Toews

> Do you think the state should have the right to intervene between a mother and a fetus? Explain.

In 1987, with the aid of brand-new technologies, we have returned to the ancient dictum that women are merely the temporary vessels in which the male seed grows.

In April of this year, an Ontario family court awarded responsibility for a fetus three months before its birth to the Ontario Children's Society. In Vancouver in May, a drug-addicted woman in labour with a breech baby was submitted to a Caesarian-section over her objections, after the attending obstetrician called a government social worker and was told the province would "apprehend" the unborn child, and to do whatever was necessary for its safety. In July, in New Westminster, BC, a male fetus was made a ward of the province. The next day it was delivered by Caesarian-section, two weeks premature.

These three cases present the very real danger that pregnant women could lose control of their bodies because the state feels it has the right to enforce "quality control" of the product of that pregnancy.

Technologies such as ultrasound, amniocentesis and chorionic villus sampling all allow careful monitoring of a fetus, which provides pregnant women the opportunity to make important medical and personal decisions and plans. However, the ability to make the walls of the womb disappear seems to have made the woman herself disappear in the perceptions of some. In such a view the fetus becomes not only an individual patient but also a more valuable person, to be protected at any cost—even at the cost of women's right to control their own bodies. And this view became legal precedent, despite the fact that a fetus is not a person, nor a woman's body a place, under current Canadian law.

If another attempt to include embryos in the Charter succeeds, we can envision everything from Pregnancy Licenses (complete with an ability-to-nurture test administered by the Pregnancy Control Commission of each province), to the Unborn Child Protection Agency (with civil servants overseeing mandatory medical/legal supervision of pregnant women including tests, drugs, and procedures as well as lifestyle/behaviour restrictions on diet, sexual activity, living arrangements, hours a day spent with feet up, etc.), to a whole new set of Labour Laws, to perhaps even the Panty Police (investigating and laying manslaughter charges if they find any of the fertilized eggs which naturally fail to attach to the uterine lining and slip out, usually undetected by the suspect).

Lest we be tempted to regard such a scenario as hysterical or paranoid, consider some recent recommendations made by the Ontario Law Reform Commission. A 1985 report suggests state regulation of motherhood, stressing that the mother's importance to the child is merely genetic; that careful "quality" screening before pregnancy and monitoring during pregnancy should be conducted; and that even such a carefully chosen mother be compelled to give up custody by court order when necessary. These measures are not now intended for all pregnant women, or even for each of those women referred to above who lost in-utero custody because she was sleeping in a garage, addicted to drugs, or described as "spacey." These laws are for that class of women who consider $10,000 a good wage for conceiving and bearing a child as a "surrogate."

While child custody laws have swung from paternity rights when children were an economic asset to maternity rights when they became a liability, many writers see the current situation not so much as a fathers' rights backlash but as evidence of individual patriarchy being superceded by state patriarchy. And with this summer's custody decisions, even the shaky ground upon which pregnant women and mothers now stand may be torn from under them if not only children but also embryos become state-owned natural resources and the women themselves merely the processors of raw materials.

—Canadian Dimension, October 1987

RESPONSE

1. Do you agree with the author's claim, "we have returned to the ancient dictum that women are merely the temporary vessels in which the male seed grows"? Explain.

2. Cite three examples from the editorial which support the claim expressed by the author in the opening sentence.

3. Explain what the author means by "individual patriarchy being superceded by state patriarchy."

EXTENSION

4. Read the Canadian Charter of Rights and write a journal entry about the rights you have as a citizen which mean the most to you.

Baby Gabriel's Gift of Life
Should it Happen Again?
Dr. Calvin Stiller, Dr. D. Alan Shewmon

Research the etymology of the word *dilemma*. What is implied in the concept of dilemma?

Recount an incident from your own life in which there was no right or wrong answer.

Last October, a three-and-a-half-day-old baby girl born in Orillia, Ont., made medical history. She had anencephaly, an invariably fatal genetic defect in which the upper portion of the brain fails to develop. Her parents, who had named her Gabriel after the biblical angel, had offered her organs for transplant. Doctors declared Gabriel brain dead when she proved unable to breathe after 10 minutes away from a respirator. Then, she was flown to a leading transplant centre in Loma Linda, Calif., where Paul Holc, son of a Surrey, B.C., couple, had been born with a fatal heart defect. Her heart saved his life. But the transplant has raised ethical questions that still haunt doctors.

PRO

Dr. Calvin Stiller is chief of transplantation at University Hospital in London, Ont.

CON

Dr. D. Alan Shewmon is a pediatric neurologist in Los Angeles.

PRO

The anencephalic, who will inevitably die within a few days (or in exceptional circumstances, weeks), is the tragic outcome of a pregnancy initiated with love and dreams. Despite the terrible malformation of the brain, this is a human child able to breathe, make movements and, in some cases, suck because the brain stem, the area that regulates breathing and vital functions, is intact. In 75 percent of all cases, the rest of the body is healthy.

Parents like Baby Gabriel's have for years sought to have some good emerge from their dashed hopes. As a physician in charge of a transplant program, I have often been approached by women expecting anencephalics. They pleaded with me to redeem their pregnancies by using those organs that could bring life and hope to other parents whose infants are born with a normal brain but a fatal defect in some other vital organ.

Until very recently, I could not help these mothers. The dilemma that I and other physicians faced was that anencephalics, with their functioning brain stems, did not meet the rigorously followed criteria for declaration of brain death. Organs are not taken from individuals until it has been determined with absolute certainty that their brain is dead. Only then can they be declared legally dead.

Some physicians, notably a group in California, had sought to get around this difficulty. In 1986, they had attempted to have anencephalics declared brain dead without the requirement for brain-stem death. They did not succeed because most physicians, myself included, found this departure from normal procedure morally objectionable.

My view was that, as long as spontaneous breathing gave evidence of brain-stem life, one could not pronounce death. Any attempt to do so would be unethical. And even if the medical community reached a consensus to declare such patients dead, their decision would be seen as expedience. Meanwhile, the need for infant organ donors was inescapable. Events that cause death without damaging transplantable organs rarely occur among babies.

The problem seemed insoluble until a group of international experts met in January 1987, in London, Ont., to review the whole issue and determine whether an ethical, morally sensitive approach could permit the use of some anencephalics as organ donors. Neurologists, pediatricians, clergy, ethicists, philosophers, lawyers and transplant experts reached a surprising consensus that paved the way for the Baby Gabriel case.

Anencephaly, we agreed, is a special category of malformation for three reasons: no mistake in diagnosis can occur, there is no hope for life, and the usual treatment is abortion—destruction of the fetus in the womb during the late stages of pregnancy or benign neglect if the child is delivered alive. We decided from the outset that the results of our deliberations on anencephaly would not apply to any other malformation, including hydrocephalus, birth injuries, genetic abnormalities and mental retardation.

We were not about to use anencephalics' organs without recognizing their humanity. When a transplant involving an anencephalic is anticipated, two concerns are paramount: the wishes of the parents and the interests of the fetus or newborn child. Pain and suffering must not occur.

We drew up specific treatment guidelines affecting every stage in an anencephalic's brief life. It is unethical to view such patients as potential organ donors unless these guidelines are strictly followed—including the accepted criteria for brain death.

With the guidelines in hand, we awaited the next plea from a mother. It reached us from Orillia last fall. The baby was maintained on a respirator, pain free, and when all evidence of brain function ceased and she was declared dead, her parents gave permission for donation of her organs.

Gabriel received the utmost respect and protection. No ethical issue was offended. No legal definitions were rewritten. The result was the saving of a newborn in Loma Linda whose death was certain, and the redemption of a pregnancy with a tragic outcome. As Gabriel's mother said, her baby accomplished more in her few days of life than most of us can hope to accomplish in a lifetime.

People ignorant of the medical details of the case have been quick to object. However, the long-term consequences of this medical experiment have yet to be determined. Only after additional cases, critical analysis of the specific facts in each one, adjudication by experts and ultimate acceptance by society will we truly understand the benefits of this procedure. The respect shown Baby Gabriel points the way to that goal.

CON

In Robin Cook's novel, *Coma*, patients are rendered comatose and then maintained in a vegetative state indefinitely as part of a ghoulish plot for black-market trafficking in organs for transplantation. Do we want this to become a reality?

It was claimed that Baby Gabriel became "brain dead" after having been placed on a ventilator. If this diagnosis was accurate, then the fact that she had anencephaly was totally irrelevant to the ethical propriety of transplanting her organs.

As a pediatric neurologist, however, I know of no theoretical reason to expect an anencephalic to become spontaneously brain dead while on a ventilator. Rather, the ventilator ought to keep the brain stem alive just as effectively as it preserves the other organs. If, at some moment, the baby becomes unresponsive and fails to breathe spontaneously off the ventilator, this does not necessarily mean that the brain stem is dead. There could be potentially reversible causes, such as sedative pain medication, low blood sugar, abnormal salt concentration in the blood or lack of certain hormones (to all of which anencephalics are prone). But the irreversible—not merely momentary—loss of all brain functions is what is essential for a determination of death. Unless evidence for irreversibility exists, physicians should not declare death.

Given the theoretical unlikelihood that brain death would occur in the vast majority of anencephalics on ventilators, it seems unjustified automatically to place them on ventilators shortly after birth in the vague hope that somehow, sometime, they might become legitimate organ donors. This makes as little medical or ethical sense as to place patients with other terminal illnesses on ventilators without their consent, merely for the off chance that, somehow, they might become brain dead and their organs could be harvested. Such a practice would dehumanize patients, treating them as nothing more than tissue banks and subjecting them nonvoluntarily to uncomfortable medical procedures not for their own benefit and, in the majority of cases, not even for anyone else's benefit.

The birth of an anencephalic infant is a tragedy in which parents naturally search for meaning. Health professionals traditionally empathize with such parents and try to support them through the grieving process. But I feel even more sorry for parents who have been led by certain physicians into thinking that legitimate meaning can be found in offering their baby's organs even prior to natural death.

One such couple was recently quoted in the press as stating that the opponents of organ harvesting "can't tell [us] what rights [we've] got or not got. . . . As the parents of this baby, we can do what we want to do considering that the baby is doomed to die." They seem to imply that the anticipated duration of life is somehow relevant to the morality of killing.

Such parents are emotionally focused on their own particular situation, and their desire to help another child through organ donation is laudable. But we can hardly expect them, under the circumstances, to undertake an in-depth study of medical ethics or to analyze dispassionately the long-term effects on society resulting from legitimization of nonvoluntary organ removal from live disabled individuals. (Once society gets used to killing anencephalics, and a great need for organs still remains, what category of disability will be targeted next?)

Physicians who encourage well-intentioned but ethically unsophisticated parents to think along these lines do not really help them, in the long run, to find "meaning" in their tragedy. Rather, they draw them innocently into a moral quagmire that could possibly haunt them for the rest of their lives: eventually, they may begin to realize not only that they authorized the killing of their child but also that they unwittingly contributed to the transformation of society along the lines depicted in Cook's novel, *Coma*.

Although increasing organ donations is a noble goal, such nearsighted solutions will ultimately backfire by undermining the public's trust in the whole transplantation enterprise. History has documented all too often what eventually becomes of societies in which entire classes of defenceless individuals are used as work animals or as objects for the benefit of a lucky elite. Such societies inevitably disintegrate, and it is just as well that they do. The medical, legal and ethical controversies surrounding anencephalic organ donation ought to be studied thoroughly and resolved within the respective professions before we draw the distraught parents of disabled children into heartrending dilemmas that ought not to exist in the first place.

—Chatelaine, May 1988

RESPONSE

1. Establish the facts and the sequence of events in the life and death of Baby Gabriel.

2. With a partner or in a small group, write a point-form summary of each argument.

3. Determine what these two physicians have in agreement.

EXTENSION

4. In a current periodical, find an article which examines a moral or ethical dilemma. Present a summary of the article to members of your class.

Full Moons and White Men

Suzanne P. Harwood, M.D.

> Recount an incident during which you were treated unfairly because of your age. Describe your feelings at the time and the way you feel about the incident now.

I got to know Mr. Leavitt* when I was practicing cardiology at the university and he was awaiting heart surgery. He did well through the surgery, but afterward he developed a life-threatening heart rhythm. I tested a variety of drugs by monitoring his heartbeat with a 24-hour tape recorder that he wore at home. Each time he handed in a tape, I would scan it, hoping the tachycardia would not appear, and each time it would be there. Finally, a new drug cut down the number of attacks. I increased the dose, and the next tape showed the tachycardia was gone. We were so pleased.

When Mr. Leavitt caught cold two months later, his local doctor decided he was taking too much medicine and cut the new drug's dose in half. Within three days, Mr. Leavitt was dead. I called his wife to tell her how sorry I was, and her 12-year-old son answered.

"Women shouldn't be doctors. You killed him," was all he said.

I was angry at the injustice of the boy's accusation, but I'm afraid he might have been right; if his father had a male doctor, perhaps he would have lived. Perhaps the local doctor was like so many other doctors who would not call a woman for advice, and so changed the medication without calling me.

Part of my decision to leave the private practice of cardiology, which is dependent on referrals from other physicians, and to work in a hospital doing emergency medicine, came from incidents like

---

*Not his real name

this. I began to think about how I might influence people to change their prejudices.

While I was mulling this over, I overheard two doctors complaining about how difficult their weekend on call had been. Only a full moon, they insisted, could have produced so much work. Neither bothered to notice that the moon was not full.

This folklore that a full moon spells disaster is so ingrained that one of the most prestigious medical journals in the country published the results of a study tabulating admissions for medicine, for psychiatric problems, and for trauma at a large urban hospital. There was no increase in admissions during the full moon.

But it is useless to point to scientific evidence against this myth. When I quote the article to doctors, nurses, or aides, they smile. They know better.

I began to realize that the homogeneity of our lives made it easy to identify what was different: the woman doctor, the full moon. All of us on the staff were white, middle class and Christian. We knew what "normal" was. And although I was accepted and liked, I was an anomaly—doctors were white men and nurses were women of all colors.

One day, I walked over to see a new patient: a woman sitting on the edge of the stretcher waiting to have five sutures removed from her arm. I usually inspect the wound and, if it is healed, have one of the nurses remove the sutures.

I said, "Hi, I'm Dr. Harwood, Ms. Smith. How are you doing?"

She recoiled. "Oh, no," she said, "not a woman doctor. Oh, I don't want a woman doctor again."

"What's wrong with women?"

"I had a woman doctor before, and she was awful. My doctor was away, and she came to see me in the hospital. She stopped my water pill even though I was so bloated. She tried to tell me that I didn't need it. As soon as my doctor came back, I told him what she did, and he put me right back on. I don't want a woman doctor again."

"Was she white?"

"What?" She looked confused. "Well, yes."

"So, there's your problem," I said. "Avoid white doctors."

On another occasion, an ambulance call came over the speaker. They were bringing in a nine-year-old boy who had broken a chemical ice pack against his lip. He had not swallowed anything, and there was no burn, but he was coming by ambulance. The inappropriate use of ambulances is a continual annoyance to the emergency room staff. They were exasperated. One of them said, "I'll bet he's black."

When the white couple arrived with their unharmed, healthy son, it was difficult to keep a straight face. There was not the slightest redness on his lip, no sign, that I could examine. They left, and I turned to the staff. "Those whites!" I said in disgust.

We see some dirty, lying, and obnoxious patients in the emergency room, and most of them, like most of our patients, are white. I have started to point out their color—"it's those whites"—whenever I come across one of them. It's too early to tell if I am making any impact, but I haven't heard any comments against blacks since I started.

I am trying also to broaden my scope: "You know, the white, male newscaster" or "Do you know which one I mean? The fellow who starred in the movie about white boys going to school." Instead of offensive, ethnic jokes, I substitute "white doctor" for the name of the ethnic group. How many "white doctors" does it take to change a light bulb?

It pleases me. When I call my colleagues the "white, male doctor," I am reassuring myself that they are not the standard; they are just another easily identified subgroup. And if one of them happens to be a fussy, angry person who gives the nurses a hard time, I get a lot of satisfaction out of saying "those white men!" when he leaves. It seems healthy for those who have never been different to hear the label as though they were. I now have a dream: a patient is sitting in the exam room when one of my male colleagues walks in. The patient says with incredulity, "Oh! A *male* doctor!"

RESPONSE

1. What factors influenced Harwood's decision to leave private practice?

2. According to Harwood, what is the connection between the woman doctor and the full moon?

3. Explain why Harwood substitutes "white doctor" for an ethnic group in offensive jokes.

EXTENSION

4. a) Are there "identifiable subgroups" who are treated unfairly in your school?
   b) Devise a plan of action to promote more tolerance and understanding of these identifiable subgroups.

Baseball and the Facts of Life

Bob Greene

List five benefits and five drawbacks of organized amateur sport. Do the benefits outweigh the drawbacks? Explain.

He is nine years old; his name is Brett. For three years he has been asking his parents if he could play in the Little League. This summer they said yes.

He is small for his age, with curly brown hair and bright blue eyes. The girls think he is cute, but he tells his mother he doesn't care about that. When his mother and father said he could play in the league this year, he just about exploded with joy. In other summers, he watched baseball on television; this year he was going to play.

His parents took him to the first practice, and they could see it in his eyes: he idolized the man who was coaching the team. The other boys had played in years before—Little Leaguers start young—but Brett didn't care. At last he was going to be one of them.

After the first few games, he would come home from practice, and his parents could sense that something was wrong. It is best not to pry into the secrets of little boys, but they were concerned. So one night, after dinner, they walked over to see his team play.

They watched as the game started, and their son did not get in. There were fifteen boys on the team, some of them very good. But most of them were bigger than Brett, and stronger; they were the ones who played the whole game. The coach let Brett in for one inning; when the inning was over, the coach took him out.

At home, after the game, Brett's parents asked him what had been bothering him.

He said that at the beginning of the season, the coach had said that every boy would play. But for Brett, that meant only the bare minimum—one inning each game. The coach was afraid that if Brett stayed in for too long, the team might lose the game. As it was, he was put in right field, the place that boys who are not good enough are traditionally sent.

His mother started going to every game. She would watch as Brett stood on the sidelines, his eyes alive, everything in his face almost begging to get in. And every game she watched as the coach reluctantly let her son play for one inning, and not a moment more.

At home, Brett would put his uniform on four hours before he was supposed to go to the game. He would walk around the house in it, look at himself in the mirror, check the clock every few minutes; the games were scheduled to start at six p.m., but Brett would get there at quarter to five, just to be sure. Every game was going to be the one when he would really get to play.

And his mother kept going to the games. Even from a distance she could see those eyes lighting up every time it seemed he might get to go in. She would see those eyes, and then she would see the coach not even knowing her son was there. The coach looking at the more skillful boys out on the field, and her son looking at the coach; it made her feel sick to see it.

One day, after the game, when no one was looking, she approached the coach. She asked him why.

"I have to keep the best ones in," the coach said. "We're in a league, you know. We're trying to win. I have five boys on the team who only play one inning. Your son is one of them."

At home, Brett would ask his father to practice with him in the driveway.The father is not an athletically inclined man, but of course he said yes; Brett said he was "working on his arm," as if that would help change things at the next game.

And every game, he would get into his uniform early; every game, he would be the first one at the field.

His mother watched one game as he got in. The boys who got to play regularly—the skillful ones—horsed around between innings, did tricks on their bikes and made jokes with each other. Brett, though, looked only at the game. He never even got a drink of water. This night, when he got to bat, he kept in mind the coach's admonitions about not backing away from the ball. The pitch came in hard and close, and it hit him hard enough to make him cry. When the inning was over he stood expectantly on the sidelines, hoping to get back in. But the coach only called to the regulars:

"Double the limit at the Dairy Queen if you win." Brett did not play again that night.

One evening it happened: for some reason a lot of the boys had other things to do, and there were only nine present when it was time for the game to begin. His mother was there again, and she saw the coach tell Brett that he was going to get to start the game in right field. She saw him begin to smile, and then to suppress it; he ran out to right field, part of the starting team.

In the middle of the first inning, one of the regulars rode up on his bike. The coach was clearly glad to see him. When Brett trotted off the field, he saw that the other boy had arrived. The coach took Brett out; his evening was over.

The season is almost finished now. Brett does not put his uniform on four hours early anymore; he does not watch the clock. He still goes to the games, but he has learned his lesson. He doesn't talk about baseball around the house.

His parents are trying to find a moral in all of this. They know it happens to many boys in thousands of cities around the country every summer. His parents tell themselves that maybe it will turn out to be a good experience; maybe it will teach their son something about life, and about dreams, and about putting too much faith in those dreams.

That's what they tell themselves, but they don't believe it. All they know is that their son, at the age of nine, has been shown that he isn't good enough. We all learn that sometime in this life; some find it out earlier than others. The other night, Brett told his parents that he wasn't going to play baseball next summer. The eyes weren't as bright; that's what hurt his parents the most. The eyes weren't as bright.

RESPONSE

1. What does Brett want?

2. Defend or condemn the actions of the coach.

3. How responsible are Brett's parents for what happens to him? Explain.

4. Explain why you agree or disagree with the sentiments expressed in this statement: "All they know is that their son, at the age of nine, has been shown that he isn't good enough. We all learn that sometime in this life. . . ."

EXTENSION

5. Have you had, or witnessed, an experience similar to Brett's? Describe and explain the similarities between your experience and Brett's experience.

6. Write a short story about a young person's experience with competition.

Life
and
Spirit

Margaret Laurence:
A Remembrance

Timothy Findley

> Recount an incident in which a person known to you displayed courage. As a class, define courage making reference to several of these accounts.

"Mind must be the firmer,
Heart the more fierce,
Courage the greater
As our strength diminishes."

These are lines from an old English poem that was cherished by Margaret Laurence—cherished, rehearsed over time and implemented. Wherever she found these words—whenever it was they first refused to go away and leave her alone—that moment must be counted as one of the most important in all the sixty years of her life. As words—as articulation—they became a cornerstone of her resources. They inform not only her writing: they also inform whatever we know of how she lived and how she died.

Margaret Laurence was a great believer in simplicity. She was also one of its greatest practitioners. This is where the *firmness* came in. Firmness—for Margaret Laurence—was one of simplicity's most important synonyms. *I will* and *I won't* were two of her absolutes. She would not and could not tolerate anything less than her full capacity to make words work on paper. Nor would she tolerate anything less than her full capacity to stand for what she believed in.

As time progressed—and her capacities expanded—she also progressed from *firm* to *firmer*. If you knew Margaret Laurence, you had to contend with this sometimes difficult part of her will. And if you knew her well, you wished, in a way, you could protect her from it. Part of her firmness—and, of course, an extremely potent part of her will—was her rejection, which was *total*, of any kind of safety: personal, intellectual or physical. She struggled thirty years and more at her table to produce on the page an account of what was in her mind—and that, as any serious writer knows, is a struggle utterly without the benefit of self-preservation. The onslaught of fictional men and women, ideas and events—all of whom and all of which can achieve their existence only if the writer succeeds at giving them articulation—has a strange, seductive power to suggest that articulation "cannot be achieved." Unless you are firm.

So Margaret Laurence stayed there at her table, no matter how long it took to get things right. And when she rose and when she handed over what she had written, she said: "this is it—the way it should be—the way it must be—the way it is and the way it will stay."

This is it: the way it will stay: *The Stone Angel—A Jest of God—The Fire Dwellers—A Bird In The House—The Diviners* ... Firm—firmer—firmest.

The fierceness in her was mighty.

Margaret Laurence had to contend with a body whose nervous system tended to betray her just when she needed it most to be strong. She shook. Her knees gave way. Her hands could be seen from almost any distance, reaching for the backs of chairs and the tops of tables—anything to hold her up and stop her from shaking. Rising to speak—choosing, against all odds, to rise at all—in order to tell what she believed—these were the harshest enemies she had whenever it came to speaking her mind. But speak her mind she must, and fiercely. She said something once that gave the essence of all her beliefs: her certainty that we, her beloved humankind, were capable of willful, self-determined sanity if only we would *try* ... Margaret Laurence believed, with a passion so profound it almost puts me to shame to think of it, that war and hatred must *and can* be put aside. And she devoted, even to the point of exhaustion, all the latter years of her life to activities supporting this belief. But her open espousal of peace through nuclear disarmament brought her, as it must, a host of enemies, name-callers, finger-pointers: people who called her a "fool," a "red" and the word that disturbed her most—"subversive." What Margaret Laurence said to these accusers was said with the kind of ferocity that only absolute certainty can justify. "If the quest for peace," she said, "is subversive—*then what, in the name of God, is war?*"

Fierce—fiercer—fiercest.

One day the word came that Margaret Laurence was going to die. No backing off; no second chance at survival; nothing to mitigate the certainty. Up to about a year before this day arrived, those of us who knew and loved her had been aware of her struggles to take up the pen again and write. Her last major piece of work had been published in 1974. This was her masterpiece: *The Diviners*. But since that year, her writer's output had been meagre: three books for children and one of essays written in the past. Her time was given over to Anti-Nuclear and Peace activities. She was also, with great success and personal popularity, the Chancellor of Trent University. But what she wanted, besides these things, was one more book. And it wouldn't come.

What very few people knew was that, during this time, Margaret Laurence was slowly going blind with cataracts. She couldn't properly wield the pen—she couldn't properly type—though both activities were still producing a vast outpouring of letters to students and fans and friends. And then there was a "miracle." A plastic lens was implanted in one of her eyes—and she began to write again. She could barely believe her good fortune. What she wrote—and what she completed and what, in a not too distant future will be published—was a book devoted to the theme of motherhood: a Memoir. She worked on this until the week before she died.

Brave—braver—bravest.

Euripides told us: Never that which is shall die.

He didn't mean people, I guess. I guess what he meant was ideas and truths and things like that. I think he meant, too, that whatever goes into life—the whole of what is alive—is alive forever. Margaret Laurence is dead. But so, we are told, is Euripides. I'm sure you know exactly what I mean. Goodbye, Margaret Laurence. And thank you!

RESPONSE

1. a) Which of Margaret Laurence's traits does Findley most admire?
   b) What do you find most admirable about Margaret Laurence?

2. What aspects of Laurence's behaviour present a model of courage for others?

EXTENSION

3. For interest and enjoyment, read one of Margaret Laurence's novels.

4. Write a brief biography of the most courageous person known to you.

5. Write an account of the moments in your life when you are called upon to be most courageous.

The Snow Walker

Farley Mowat

To what groups in society do you feel you belong? What is the nature of the bond among the members of each group? What are the responsibilities of each member?

I am Ootek, and my people are the people of the River of Men. Once they were many and the land was good to them, but now it is my time and we have almost forgotten how it was in the old days when the deer flooded the tundra and gave us life. Hunger comes often now, and the deer but seldom. No one now lives by the big lakes to the north although when my father was young the tents of the people stood everywhere along those shores. I have travelled down the River to the big lakes but when I reached them I turned back from an empty land.

Only the spirits who remain in those places remember the times when a man might stand on a hill as the deer passed by and though he looked to the east or the west, the south or the north, he would see only their brown backs and hear only the clicking of antlers and the grumbling of their full bellies.

The great herds have gone . . . and so we who lived by the deer must follow the Snow Walker even as my father followed him in the spring of the year.

After the ice had grown thick on the lakes last winter there came a time of storms and for many days we stayed in our igloos. The children grew quiet and did not play and the old people sometimes looked toward the door tunnels with shadowed eyes. The snows mounted over the top of the igloos until we could not even venture out to look for willow twigs to burn. The igloos were cold and dark for we had long since eaten the deer fat that should have burned in the lamps. So little food remained to us from the few southbound deer we had been able to kill in the autumn that the dogs were beginning to starve, and we ourselves were not much better off.

One day Belikari, who was my closest neighbour among the seven families living in the camp, came to tell me that a mad fox had run into the tunnel of his snowhouse where his dogs lay and had bitten three of them before it was killed by the rest. Those three dogs died with foam at their lips, and they were only three of many. This was another evil because when the foxes went mad their pelts became worthless and so, even if the storms had allowed us to travel, it would have been no use visiting the traps.

After a long time the blizzards ended and the weather grew calm and cold. All the people had survived though some of the old ones could hardly stir from the sleeping ledges. We younger men took the few remaining dogs and went searching for meat we had cached on the Flat Country. We found only a little because most of the caches were buried under hard drifts that had mounted so high they had covered the markers.

The women and children helped to keep famine at bay by digging under the drifts near the igloos for fish bones and scraps of old hides with which to make soup. By such means we hoped to cling to our lives until the warm winds and the lengthening days might bring the deer back to our country from the forested lands in the south.

But long after the time when the ice should have started to rot, it still lay heavy and hard on the rivers and lakes, and the days seemed to grow colder again until we wondered if winter would ever come to an end. We ate all the food we had, and the deer did not come. We waited . . . for there was nothing else we could do. We ate the last of our dogs, and still the deer did not come.

One day the men gathered in Owliktuk's snowhouse. His wife, Kunee, sat on the ledge with her child in her arms, and the child was dead. We knew it could not be very long before many of the women were nursing such sorrow. My cousin, Ohoto, put some thoughts into words.

"Perhaps people should go away from this place now. Perhaps they might go south to the place where the white man has come to live. It might happen that he would have food he would give us."

The white man had only recently come to live on the edge of our country, to trade with us for foxes. It was a long way to his place and only Ohoto had been there before. Since we had no dogs, we knew we would have to carry everything on our backs, and the children and old people would not be able to ride on the sleds as they should. We knew some of them would not see the white man's place . . . but the child of Owliktuk and Kunee was dead. We decided to go.

The women rolled up a few skins to use for tent shelters and sleeping robes; the children carried whatever they could, and we men slung our packs on our shoulders and we left our camp by the River and set out into the south.

Soon after we started, the sun turned warm and for five days we walked up to our knees in melting snow. My wife's mother had lost count of the years she had lived, yet she walked with the rest and still helped to pitch camp at the end of each day. But on the fifth night she did not offer to help. She sat by herself with her back to a rock and spoke to none except Ilupalee, my daughter. She called the child to her.

From a distance I watched and listened as the old woman put her bony hands on my daughter's head. I heard her softly singing her spirit song to the child, the secret song she had received from her mother's mother and with which she could summon her helping spirit. Then I knew she had made up her mind what she must do.

It was her choice, and my wife and I could say nothing about it, not even to tell her of the sorrow we felt. During the night, she went from the camp. None saw her go. We did not speak her name after that for one may not use the name of a person who has gone out on the land to seek the Snow Walker until the name and the spirit it bears can be given again to a newly born child.

The next day we reached the Little Stick country which borders the forests. Here there was plenty of wood so we could at least have fires where we could warm ourselves. Toward evening we overtook Ohoto's family squatted beside a fire, melting water to drink since there was no food. Ohoto told me his daughter had fallen and could not rise again so they had to make camp. When the rest of the people came up, it was clear that many, both young and old, could not go on; and Ohoto thought we were still two or three days distant from the home of the white man.

I had been carrying Ilupalee on my shoulders most of the day and was so tired I could not think. I lay down by the fire and shut my eyes. Ilupalee lay beside me and whispered in my ear:

"A white hare is sitting behind the little trees over there."

I thought this was only a dream born out of hunger so I did not open my eyes. But she whispered again:

"It is a big, fat hare. She Who Walked said it was there."

This time I opened my eyes and got to my knees. I looked where she pointed and could see nothing except a patch of dwarf spruce. All the same I unslung the rifle from my pack and walked toward the trees.

Indeed it was there!

But one hare does not provide more than a mouthful of food for twenty-five people so we had to think carefully what should be done. It was decided that the three strongest men—Alekahaw, Ohoto and I—would eat the hare and thereby gain strength to go on to the white man's place. My wife built a fire apart from the camp so the others would not have to endure the smell of meat cooking. She boiled the hare and we three men shared it; but we left the guts, bones, skin and the head to make soup for the children.

We walked away from the camp along a frozen stream so we would not have to wade through the soft snow. My skin boots were thin and torn and my feet were soon numb because at each step we broke through the thin crust above the thaw water. I did not mind because my stomach was warm.

It was growing dark on the second day when we came to a clearing in a spruce woods on the shore of a lake where the white man had his house. His dogs heard us and howled and when we came near he opened the door and waited with the bright light of a lamp shining behind him. We stopped and stood where we were because he was a stranger, and a white man, and we had met very few white men. He spoke to us, but not in our language, so we could not reply. When he spoke again, very loudly, and still we did not reply, he went back into his house.

It grew cold as the darkness settled around us, and our wet boots became stiff as they froze. I thought of Ilupalee and wanted very much to do something, but did not know what we should do.

After a long time the door opened again and the white man came out. He was wiping his beard. We smelled hot fat from his house but he shut the door behind him and motioned us to follow him to another small cabin.

He unlocked the door and we went in. He lit a lamp and hung it on a rafter so we could see that the walls were piled high with boxes, but we looked hardest at the many bags of flour stacked in front of a table. We started to smile for we believed the white man understood our needs and would help us. We stood under the lamp watching the flame reflect light from the beads of cold fat still clinging to the white man's beard, and we gave ourselves up to the joy growing within us.

The white man opened a drawer in the table and took out a handful of small sticks of the kind used to show how much a trapper can have in exchange for the fox pelts he brings. Holding these sticks in his hand he spoke sharply in his own tongue. When we did not reply he went to a wall of the cabin, took down a fox pelt and laid it before us; then he pointed to the carrying bags which were slung on our shoulders.

The joy went out of us then. I made signs to show we had no fox pelts to trade, and Alekahaw opened his bag to show how empty it was. The white man's eyes were of a strange green colour and I could not look into them. I looked at his forehead instead while I waited for whatever must happen. Slowly his face grew red with anger, then he threw the sticks back in the drawer and began to shout at us.

Anger is something we fear since an angry man may do foolish and dangerous things. When I saw the anger in this man's face, I backed to the door. I wanted to go from that place but Alekahaw was braver than me. He stood where he was and tried to explain to the white man how it was at the camp where the rest of the people were starving. He pulled up his *holiktu* so the man could see for himself how Alekahaw's ribs stuck out from his body. Alekahaw touched his own face to show how tightly the skin was stretched over the bones.

The white man shrugged his shoulders. Perhaps he did not understand. He began turning down the flame in the lamp and we knew he would soon go back to his house, then the door would be shut against the needs of the people. Quickly Ohoto pulled two boxes of shells out of his bag. These were the last bullets he had and he had been saving them against the time when the deer would return. Now he put them on the table and pointed to the flour.

The white man shook his head. He was still angry. He picked up the lamp and started to go to the door. Alekahaw and Ohoto stepped out of his way, but something happened inside me and although I was frightened I would not let him pass.

He kept his eyes on me but he stretched out one hand behind him until it came to rest on a rifle hung on the wall. I could not make way for him then because I was afraid to move while he had his hand on that gun.

So we all stood still for a while. At last he picked up a small sack of flour and threw it over the table to fall at Ohoto's feet. Then he took the rifle, shoved me aside with the barrel, pushed the door open and told us to leave. We went outside and watched as he locked the door. We watched as he went back into his house.

A little while later we saw him looking out of his window. He still had the rifle in his hand so we knew there was no use remaining. We walked away into the darkness.

Day was breaking when we got back to the camp. Those who were still able to stand gathered in front of Owliktuk's tent and we told what we had to tell. We showed them the sack of flour which was so small a child could easily lift it.

Owliktuk spoke against us, blaming us because we had not taken the food that was needed. He said we could have repaid the white man next winter when the foxes were again good. But if we had tried to take food from the white man there would have been killing. Perhaps Owliktuk only spoke as he did because his second child was now going from him. The rest of the people said nothing but returned to their families with the small portions of flour which were their shares.

I carried my father's share to his tent. Although he had once been the best hunter among us and only the previous year had fathered a child on his third wife, he had aged very much during the winter and his legs had weakened until he could barely walk. When I told him what had happened and gave him the flour for himself, my stepmother and the small child, he smiled and said, "One has a son who knows what may be done and what may not be done. One is glad no blood was shed. It may be that things will get better."

It did not seem he was right about that. We had made the journey to the white man's place and it had come to so little. Now we were too weak to go back to our own land. And on the second day after we three men returned to the camp, the Snow Walker came to the children Aljut and Uktilohik. There was no mourning for them because those who still lived had no sorrow to spend on the dead.

Each day thereafter the sun shone more brightly. Spring was upon us and still the deer had not returned. One day I tried to visit my father to see how it was with him but I was unable to walk that short distance. I crawled back into my own tent where my wife sat rocking herself with her eyes closed and her mouth wide and gasping. Beside her my daughter sometimes wailed in the thin, dry voice of an old woman. I lay down on some brush inside the flap and together we waited.

Perhaps it was the next day when I awakened to hear someone shout. The shout came again and the voice seemed familiar and the words set my heart racing.

"Here is a deer!"

I caught my rifle by the muzzle and crawled into the morning sunlight. At first I was blinded but after a moment I saw a fine buck standing a little way off with his head high, watching the camp.

I raised my rifle with hands that could not seem to hold it. The sights wavered and the deer seemed to slide up and down the barrel. Clutching it tight, I took aim and fired. The buck flung up his forefeet and leapt toward the sheltering trees. I fired again and again until the rifle was empty but the shots all went wide. I could see them kicking up little spouts of snow but I could not hear the hard thud that tells a hunter when he has hit.

The deer ran away . . . but just when it was about to disappear in the trees it stumbled and fell. With all my strength I willed it not to get up. The deer's spirit struggled with mine until slowly the buck sank on his side.

Some of the people had come out into the sunlight and with weak voices were asking each other who had been shooting.

"Get out your knives!" I cried as loud as I could. "One has killed a fat deer!"

At my words even those who could not walk found enough strength. People wept as they stumbled and staggered toward the deer carcass. The first ones to reach it clung to it like flies, sucking the blood that still bubbled out of its wound. They moved away after a while to make room for others, sobbing with pain and holding their hands to their bellies.

The women sliced into the carcass with their round knives and tore out the entrails, snatching at the little scraps of white fat that clung to the guts. The men cut off the legs at the lower joints and cracked the bones to get at the marrow. In only a short time the buck was changed into a pile of bones, steaming meat and red snow.

It grew warm under the sun and some people began returning to the shelters with meat for those who were too weak to move. Then I remembered that I had seen no one from the tent of my father, so I made my way there dragging part of a forequarter. The flap was down over the door but I pushed it aside and crawled in. My stepmother was lying under a piece of hairless old hide and she was holding her child against her dry dugs. Although they scarcely breathed they were both still alive. But of my father there was no sign.

I cut off a piece of meat, chewed it soft then pushed it into my stepmother's mouth and rubbed her neck till she swallowed. Then I took my little stepbrother to Ohoto's shelter, which was not far away, and Ohoto's wife made blood soup and fed the child with it while I went back to my father's place and chewed more meat for my stepmother. Before I left her, she was able to eat by herself but she could not yet talk so I did not know where my father had gone.

When I returned to my own place, I found my wife had roasted some ribs and boiled the deer's tongue. Ilupalee lay wrapped in a fresh piece of deerskin and it was good to hear her whimper with the pain of a full belly. That whole night we passed in eating and by the next day nothing of the buck remained for the ravens and foxes. The bones had been crushed and boiled for their fat, the skull had been opened and cleaned, and even the hooves had been made into soup. The strength of the buck had passed into the people and we were ready to return to our country.

Next day when I went to my father's tent my stepmother was able to stand. I told her that she and the child would now come and live in my tent, then I said, "One looks about but does not see one's father."

"*Eeee*," she replied. "He would not eat the flour you brought. He gave it to me and the child. Afterwards he went on the land to meet the Snow Walker."

A little while later I told Ohoto about the voice I had heard. No one else had heard it and none of the people in the camp except me had known there was a deer nearby. Together Ohoto and I followed the marks where my father had stumbled down to the river, then crawled north on the ice. His tracks disappeared at a bend where the current had opened a hole, but close by we found the tracks of a deer. We followed the tracks until they circled back to the camp and came to an end at the place where I had killed the big buck.

Neither Ohoto nor I said anything but we both knew whose voice I had heard.

In the autumn my wife will give birth to another child, and then the name of him who went to meet the Snow Walker that we might continue to live will surely be spoken again by the River of Men.

RESPONSE

1. Who is the Snow Walker?

2. Explain why Ootek's father and mother-in-law go to meet the Snow Walker.

3. Should the white man have given food and other essentials to Ootek and his people? Explain.

4. Should Ootek and his companions have taken what they needed from the white man? Explain.

5. What is the importance to the story of the way Ootek found and killed the deer?

EXTENSION

6. List and discuss the ways in which the values of Ootek's people differ from yours.

7. Examine several examples of Inuit painting and sculpture. What can be deduced about Inuit values from these art works?

Larry Walters, My Hero

Robert Fulghum

> Have you ever felt compelled to do something out of the ordinary? What was it? Did you go through with it? If not, what prevented you from doing it?

Now let me tell you about Larry Walters, my hero. Walters is a truck driver, thirty-three years old. He is sitting in his lawn chair in his backyard, wishing he could fly. For as long as he could remember, he wanted to go *up*. To be able to just rise right up in the air and see for a long way. The time, money, education, and opportunity to be a pilot were not his. Hang gliding was too dangerous, and any good place for gliding was too far away. So he spent a lot of summer afternoons sitting in his backyard in his ordinary old aluminum lawn chair—the kind with the webbing and rivets. Just like the one you've got in your backyard.

The next chapter in this story is carried by the newspapers and television. There's old Larry Walters up in the air over Los Angeles. Flying at last. Really getting UP there. Still sitting in his aluminum lawn chair, but it's hooked on to forty-five helium-filled surplus weather balloons. Larry has a parachute on, a CB radio, a six-pack of beer, some peanut butter and jelly sandwiches, and a BB gun to pop some of the balloons to come down. And instead of being just a couple of hundred feet over his neighborhood, he shot up eleven thousand feet, right through the approach corridor to the Los Angeles International Airport.

Walters is a taciturn man. When asked by the press why he did it, he said: "You can't just sit there." When asked if he was scared, he answered: "Wonderfully so." When asked if he would do it again, he said: "Nope." And asked if he was glad that he did it, he grinned from ear to ear and said: "Oh, yes."

The human race sits in its chair. On the one hand is the message that says there's nothing left to do. And the Larry Walterses of the earth are busy tying balloons to their chairs, directed by dreams and imagination to do their thing.

The human race sits in its chair. On the one hand is the message that the human situation is hopeless. And the Larry Walterses of the earth soar upward knowing anything is possible, sending back the message from eleven thousand feet: "I did it, I really did it. I'm FLYING!"

It's the spirit here that counts. The time may be long, the vehicle may be strange or unexpected. But if the dream is held close to the heart, and imagination is applied to what there is close at hand, everything is still possible.

But wait! Some cynic from the edge of the crowd insists that human beings still *can't really* fly. Not like birds, anyway. True. But somewhere in some little garage, some maniac with a gleam in his eye is scarfing vitamins and mineral supplements, and practicing flapping his arms faster and faster.

RESPONSE

1. What do you think about what Larry Walters did?

2. What did Larry Walters mean when he said, "You can't just sit there"?

3. According to Fulghum, what is heroic about Larry Walters?

EXTENSION

4. Tell your family the story of Larry Walters. Note their responses. Is there a "Larry Walters story" in your family? Write the story and read it to members of your class.

No, Virginia, sorry. . . .

Margaret Visser

> Do you think that society is fair to children in perpetuating the myth of Santa Claus? Do parents have a choice in perpetuating the myth of Santa Claus?
>
> Does Santa Claus fulfill specific needs for both adults and children?

The modern version of him first took shape in New York City in 1822. He was very small indeed at that date, an elf in fact, who fitted with ease into the narrowest chimney stack. He flew through the air in a sleigh full of toys, drawn by reindeer who could land on rooftops. His clothes, which covered him from head to foot in fur, were understandably begrimed with soot. He was a heavy smoker.

The elf grew into a giant as the years passed; he gave up his pipe and became cleaner and cleaner. He started to dress in gnomes' red outfits, gnomes' caps, and a broad leather belt and boots. He had been bearded from the start, and the fur of his coat—now a lining merely—became snow-white to match his hair. He used to chuckle quietly, gripping his pipe between his teeth, shaking his round belly, and presumably wheezing a bit; but later on he took to roaring with laughter—rather mirthlessly but very loud.

There is no story at all. Just a workshop for making toys at the North Pole, a few anecdotes about one of his reindeer, and that's about it. We once heard his wife mentioned occasionally, but she has been forgotten, swallowed up (metaphorically, of course) by him; several writers for psychiatric journals say he now has markedly androgynous features.

He is not a myth (myths require stories); he is a symbol, an image, a personification. He has become a benevolent figure, symbolizing aspects of the season: gift-giving, lots of fun and food, and children above all. Christmas is an old feast, and vigorous, like him.

In him Christmas is opposed to New Year's. That is to say, he is for family, domesticity, and children; New Year's is for singles, and raucous parties away from home. He rewards past good behaviour (he *knows* if you've been bad, but he never takes it out on you), whereas New Year's brings sober resolutions for the future.

There is no question that he is a fertility figure—abundance, fatness, generosity, babies. (In his bad old days that partiality for babies often meant that he enjoyed eating them.) He is obviously phallic: dressed in red, coming down the chimney, and leaving a present in the stocking. Some analysts have suspected that he is, at the same time, pregnant.

His presents are for all children, but only for children. Gift-giving can often be construed as requiring some sort of return: a thing or a service of equal value to the original gift, if not something in kind. But here is an occasion for giving on one side and simple receiving on the other: the giant gnome takes off too fast for any recompense. Adults simply watch and enjoy the pleasure given.

The Christmas crib has contributed other details: the old man bringing gifts to a child, coming down from heaven at night, arriving complete with animals and so on.

But the old man is also a superb business proposition, obligingly embodying everything about Christmas that is useful in a big store. Not being religious, he can cheerfully shoulder the task of encouraging and glorifying consumerism, and so allow people who are busy shopping to bypass the crib, the birth narrative, the poor, salvation, and God.

He operates, of course, hand-in-glove with parents; in fact, he would not be around without their help. It really is a lot of work keeping it all up: the children informed, their expectations built up, then gratified. Why do we do it?

Well, for one thing our parents did it to us, and we remember. Other parents are doing it for their children, and our child must not be left out. And parents love it: the excitement, opening the presents, the whole atmosphere—it enables them not only to be generous but to relive, through their children, the days long ago, before they themselves found out.

One of the things we all remember, don't we, is the day we found out. Someone told us—we overheard—we suddenly realized.

We did our best not to show disappointment, of course—we might even have pretended for a while we didn't know, for the sake of younger siblings, or even to keep our parents happy. This was growing up; we had to take it "like a man," show that we were not really surprised, that we didn't especially care.

And this is of course why he's there: set up for children to see through, when they are ready. He is an ingenious initiation device, whose vanishing marks the line between innocence and "the age of reason." In this rite of passage there is no revelation, only demystification.

No guide is provided for the initiate either: she is left to find out the truth, *for herself.* All of a sudden she learns many things: that parents are *not* always what they seem, that she should greet information with caution at all times, and never again expect kindness just because she exists.

RESPONSE

1. Do you think Visser is accurate in her analysis of the meaning of Santa Claus? Why or why not?

2. Do you agree that Santa Claus "can cheerfully shoulder the task of encouraging and glorifying consumerism"? Explain.

EXTENSION

3. Write a story about the day "you found out."

4. Do you think the image of Santa Claus will continue to change in response to society's needs? If so, what kinds of changes do you foresee?

Homecoming

Garrison Keillor

Recount an event of special importance to you which, through no fault of your own, became a fiasco.

It has been a quiet week in Lake Wobegon. It was Homecoming on Friday, the Leonards vs. Bowlus Friday night at Bowlus—an away game, on account of Leonard Field has developed a sinkhole about ten feet in diameter that suddenly sank two feet between the ten- and twenty-yard lines, not that the team used that part of the field very often. Coach Magendanz and Mr. Halvorson decided to fill it with clay, and found that filling it made it sink deeper, and removing the fill made it deeper yet. So they are keeping the hole under observation and Homecoming had to be moved to another location.

The parade was in town, though, and the Homecoming dance last night, reigned over by Queen Carla and King Jim, royalty elected by the senior class under the supervision of Mrs. Hoffarth, who eliminates inappropriate candidates. The drawback of secret ballots is the tendency on the part of a few to vote for the wrong person when nobody is looking, and once a girl other than the Queen got more votes for Queen, but those were not informed votes. The voters didn't know what Mrs. Hoffarth knew, or else they didn't have the best interests of Lake Wobegon High School at heart. The girl in question had been to the gravel pit, parked in a car with a boy and drinking beer, and Mrs. Hoffarth maintains that when you've been to the gravel pit, you shouldn't expect to wear a tiara and ride a convertible down Main Street. A Queen should be above gravel-pit business. "If you climb down off the pedestal, don't expect to climb back up," she says. "A pedestal is not an elevator."

For years, ever since I was in school, because Mrs. Hoffarth's brother Gerald is a colonel of the National Guard, the Homecoming Queen has ridden on a Sherman tank borrowed from the Fighting 308th armory in Freeport. She rides in the forward hatch, below the cannon, and a squad of Guardsmen march in front of her. It made a deep impression on me to see a beautiful classmate in a pink gown smiling and waving from a tank and may have warped my feelings about women, particularly beautiful ones. I talk to them and hear bolts slam in the carbines and combat boots scrape on the pavement. Fear of death isn't the best basis for a friendship. It's an okay basis, but not the best. But that is personal stuff I never told anyone, so keep it under your hat—I don't want to be asked about it by every amateur psychiatrist in town. It's a little odd thing in my makeup that comes from coming where I'm from, no stranger than thinking about death every time you put on clean underwear, one of those quirks a person can live with.

What's hard to live with is not the trash floating in your head but the ordinary facts of life: mortality, knowing that you'll die, and frailty, knowing that when we've got it figured out we don't, and indignity, knowing that if we manage to put up a good front we still have the backstage view. I suppose that's why I don't go home for Homecoming. They know stories about me that I can't explain away and call me by a nickname that I left home in order to lose. Wild horses couldn't drag it out of me now. But I'll tell you: it was Foxfart.

The Queen of Homecoming, Carla Krebsbach, has no odd nicknames to escape, no humiliating secrets, and she made a terrific Queen. She looked like a million dollars, wearing a white spangled dress you could get married in if you wanted, but with a dress like that, why get married and ruin your good looks? The soft contacts made her eyes glisten. She had her hair cut so her posture is improved. When Mrs. Hoffarth walked slowly across the stage holding up the tiara and the other four girls in line squeezed their eyes shut, Carla looked straight ahead, as if she knew for a fact whose head was going to be crowned. Hers. When it was, she didn't cry or hop up and down, she looked as if she was *ready*. The tiara dropped on her and it fit like Cinderella's glass slipper. She blinked and smiled a smile you could feel in the back row of the auditorium.

Unfortunately, her dad, Carl, couldn't be there to see it. He was at his folks' house, Myrtle and Florian's, south of town, looking into the matter of their septic tank, which had reached an emergency status the night before. Florian noticed a problem last week when he raised the extension ladder and climbed up to install storm windows. He climbed up seven rungs and was only two feet off the ground. The lawn was soft as a trampoline, and the ladder sank down into it. "Well, it'll freeze soon, and then I can get around to it," he thought, but it didn't freeze soon enough. Thursday morning the ground around the ladder had sunk three feet. "Well," he thought, "these things happen." He could put in roses there. A sunken garden. Be quite attractive. Friday morning the toilet overflowed, an event that he dared not overlook. So he called Carl.

People often call Carl in this sort of situation. It's what comes from being handy. Sometimes he envies the incompetent. He inspected the sinkhole, went back to town and borrowed the backhoe from Bud, and came back and started digging.

Even he was surprised by what he found. It appeared at first to be—and as he went deeper it actually turned out to be—a 1937 Chevy coupe that someone had buried there to use as a septic tank. Whether they couldn't afford a concrete one or just had a low opinion of that car, there it was in its subterranean glory, the roof caved in, the passenger compartment pretty well loaded to capacity.

You'll notice how gracefully I tell this story, slipping elegantly around the unnecessary or too-vivid details, touching only the high points, but I must tell you that Carl moved the backhoe around upwind and went at it from there. It had to come out—that was the only spot for a new tank unless he wanted to cut down two oak trees or put a new tank uphill of the house, which isn't the textbook way—so he hauled out this monstrosity, getting more and more curious to know who had put it there. Florian has owned the place since Carl's grandpa died. Florian had gone to town with Myrtle to watch Homecoming. Carl loaded the Chevy onto a hay wagon and didn't bother to tie it down: if it fell off, it fell off. He hitched up to the tractor and started his lonely drive to the dump, on the other side of town. By then he was not in a good humor. "Honor thy father and thy mother," yes, but did it include this? Hauling away thirty years of family history? The Chevy septic tank had lost most of its load but with the wind at his back it was suffocating.

That may have been why he didn't ask himself why so many cars were parked along McKinley Street. He didn't see a soul around and figured the coast was clear—he wasn't getting much oxygen to his brain, only the fumes of his heritage. He chugged past the high school and the Lutheran church and had to make a right turn to get the wind off his back, because now his eyes were full of tears. He hung an emergency right onto Main Street, and suddenly he was a feature attraction.

The entire population was lined up three deep on either side of Main between McKinley and Taft, and straight ahead and coming his way was the marching band and the tank behind it. The other tank.

He imagined he could make it to Taft and turn left and avoid the parade, but the old Farmall didn't have much acceleration with that load of Chev, and he and the National Guard put on the brakes and met nose to nose directly in front of the Chatterbox Cafe. The band had melted away to the side. About half the crowd began to move off toward a more distant vantage point, and the other half followed them. A strong aroma of Chev got in the ventilator of the Cafe, and the patrons silently put down their forks and emerged from the rear. Queen Carla sat on the front of the tank, her eyes almost level with her father's where he sat, in front of the old family heirloom. "How could you do this to me?" Her lips formed the words.

She was a Queen. When Queen Victoria once noticed pieces of toilet paper floating in the Thames and asked what they were, one of her counselors, the privy counselor perhaps, said, "Madam, those are printed notices saying that swimming is forbidden." Rank has its privileges, and one of them is ignorance.

The tank couldn't turn around there, the sergeant told Carl, so he had to turn the tractor and wagon. Backward and forward, backward and forward, back and up and back, and now people were cheering and clapping. First gear, reverse, first, reverse, first, reverse. Damn. Damn. Damn. Damn. "If this falls off," he thought, "I'm going to leave it and leave town." The band began to play again, "Anchors Aweigh." When the Farmall got turned around, the band fell in behind it and the three units paraded north to the statue of the Unknown Norwegian, where the second and third units turned left. The Unknown watched the Krebsbach float chug off to the dump.

In a way, it was the most memorable Homecoming ever. Graduates who heard about it later wished they had been there, because of course it won't be repeated. It was a one-time event. Which was how Carl looked at it hours later, when he'd taken a bath and was sitting in the Sidetrack enjoying a cold Wendy's. He said, "Well, if

it had to happen, I'm glad it happened where everyone could see it."
That's how I feel. Who needs dignity when you can be in show
business?

RESPONSE

1. Discuss the various implications of the following sentences as they apply
   to the story, and to life in general:
   a) "A pedestal is not an elevator."
   b) "Fear of death isn't the best basis for a friendship."
   c) "What's hard to live with is not the trash floating in your head but the
      ordinary facts of life. . . ."
   d) " . . . if we manage to put up a good front we still have the backstage
      view."
   e) "Rank has its privileges, and one of them is ignorance."
   f) "Who needs dignity when you can be in show business?"

EXTENSION

2. Compose a short story about a humorous event which involved a member
   of your family.

3. Imagine you were a spectator at the parade in *Homecoming*. Write a letter
   to a friend recounting the events of the parade.

Public Policy

Mister Blink

Michel Tremblay

> Would you ever consider running for an elected position? Why or why not?
>
> What do you think are the necessary character traits for a politician?

Mister Blink was dumbfounded. What kind of a game was this? Who had dared. . . . In front of him, on the wooden wall that ran along Cedar Street, was a huge poster, and from the middle of this poster Mister Blink smiled back at himself. Above his photograph, in violent red lettering a foot high, was an incredible sentence that startled Mister Blink: *Vote Blink, candidate of the future!*

Mister Blink removed his glasses and wiped them nervously. He put them back on his nose and looked at the poster again.

He was frightened. He started to run, and jumped onto the first bus to come by. "Impossible, it's impossible," Mister Blink said to himself. "I was dreaming, I must have been! Me, a candidate?"

For weeks people had been talking about these elections. They would surely be the most important elections of the century. One thing was certain, the two major parties were going to fight it out to the death.

Mister Blink was trembling. He tried to read his paper, but he couldn't concentrate on the little black letters that seemed to swarm like crazed flies.

For weeks people had talked about these elections. "Come on, I must have been mistaken!" The most important elections of the century. Without a doubt the most important elections of the century. "It's a joke." The most important. . . . Suddenly he cried out. In the centre-fold of his paper was the biggest picture he had ever seen in a newspaper, right in the middle, spread over the whole page. There he was. There was Mister Blink, and he was smiling, at himself. *Vote Blink, candidate of the future!* He folded his paper and threw it out the window.

Directly across from him a little boy leaned over to his mother and said, "Mommy, look, the man in the poster!" Recognizing Mister Blink, the little boy's mother jumped up and rushed at the poor man, who thought he would die of fear. "Mister Blink," exclaimed the lady as she seized his hands, "Mister Blink, our saviour!" She kissed Mister Blink's hands, and he seemed about to have a fit. "Come now, dear lady," he blurted out finally, "I am not your saviour." But the woman was already screaming as if she were quite mad, "Long live Mister Blink, our saviour!" All the people in the bus repeated together, "Long live Mister Blink. . . ."

At his neighbourhood drugstore Mister Blink bought a bottle of aspirin. "So, going into politics now, are you?" said the druggist. He wore a blue ribbon pinned to his lapel, with lettering in red. . . .

The super's wife stopped him. "Mister Blink," she said, "you wouldn't by any chance have an extra ticket for your big convention tonight, would you?" Mister Blink almost tripped back down the few steps he had just climbed. Convention? What convention? Come on now, there wasn't any convention! "Oh you are the secretive one! I should have known important things were going on in that head of yours. You can bet you sure surprised us, me and my husband."

That evening Mister Blink had no supper. If he had wanted to eat he would not have been able. The phone didn't stop ringing. His supporters wanted to know when he would get to the convention hall. Mister Blink thought he would go mad. He took the phone off the hook, put out the lights in his apartment, put on his pyjamas and went to bed.

The crowd demanded their saviour with great shouting in the street. They even threatened to break down his door if he didn't open it within ten minutes. Then the super's wife said a terrible thing that almost started a riot: "Mister Blink may be sick," she said to a journalist. Ten seconds later the crowd had knocked down his door and was triumphantly carrying off its saviour in his pyjamas. What an original outfit! It was a fine publicity stunt. A few men even went home to slip on their own pyjamas. Women in night-gowns went into the streets and followed the procession, intoning hymns of praise. Mister Blink was stunned and could not budge as he sat on the shoulders of the two most respected journalists in the country.

The convention was a smash. Mister Blink did not speak.

The new party, the people's party, Mister Blink's party burst upon the political scene like a bombshell. The old parties got only cat-calls. Slavery was abolished, thanks to Mister Blink. B-L-I-N-K. Blink! Blink! Blink! Hurrah! No more tax hikes, Mister Blink would see to that. No more increases in the cost of living. Blink! Blink! Blink!

Only once did Mister Blink attempt to stand and say something. But the crowd cheered so much he was afraid of provoking them and sat down again.

They plied him with champagne, and in the end Mister Blink agreed he was a great hero. As a souvenir of this memorable evening, Mister Blink took home a huge pennant on which, in two-foot letters. . . .

The next day Mister Blink was elected Prime Minister.

RESPONSE

1. Why do people so readily support Mister Blink?

2. In what sense is Mister Blink "a great hero"?

3. What comments does this story make on the electoral system regarding:
   a) political parties,
   b) the media,
   c) the voter?

EXTENSION

4. Imagine you are a participant in an election campaign. Form a group to write a two-minute campaign speech. Select one member of the group to rehearse and record the speech on videotape. Arrange for another class to view the videotaped campaign speeches. Poll the class to determine which speech they found most effective and why.

The Flying Machine

Ray Bradbury

> Discuss specific inventions designed to benefit humankind but which, in fact, did not.

In the year A.D. 400, the Emperor Yuan held his throne by the Great Wall of China, and the land was green with rain, readying itself toward the harvest, at peace, the people in his dominion neither too happy nor too sad.

Early on the morning of the first day of the first week of the second month of the new year, the Emperor Yuan was sipping tea and fanning himself against a warm breeze when a servant ran across the scarlet and blue garden tiles, calling, "Oh, Emperor, Emperor, a miracle!"

"Yes," said the Emperor, "the air *is* sweet this morning."

"No, no, Your Excellency."

"Let me guess then—the sun has risen and a new day is upon us. Or the sea is blue. *That* now is the finest of all miracles."

"Excellency, a man is flying!"

"What?" The Emperor stopped his fan.

"I saw him in the air, a man flying with wings. I heard a voice call out of the sky, and when I looked up, there he was, a dragon in the heavens with a man in its mouth, a dragon of paper and bamboo, coloured like the sun and the grass."

"It is early," said the Emperor. "Drink some tea. It must be a strange thing, if it is true, to see a man fly. You must have time to think of it, even as I must have time to prepare myself for the sight."

They drank tea.

"Please," said the servant at last, "or he will be gone."

The Emperor rose thoughtfully. "Now you may show me what you have seen."

They walked into a garden, across a meadow of grass, over a small bridge, through a grove of trees, and up a tiny hill.

"There!" said the servant.

The Emperor looked into the sky.

And in the sky, laughing so high that you could hardly hear him laugh, was a man; and the man was clothed in bright papers and reeds to make wings and a beautiful tail, and he was soaring all about like the largest bird in a universe of birds, like a new dragon in a land of ancient dragons.

The man called down to them from high in the cool winds of morning, "I fly, I fly!"

The servant waved to him. "Yes, yes!"

The Emperor Yuan did not move. Instead he looked at the Great Wall of China now taking shape out of the farthest mist in the green hills, that splendid snake of stones which writhed with majesty across the entire land. That wonderful wall which had protected them for a timeless time from enemy hordes and preserved peace for years without number. He saw the town, nestled to itself by a river and a road and a hill, beginning to waken.

"Tell me," he said to his servant, "has anyone else seen this flying man?"

"I am the only one, Excellency," said the servant, smiling at the sky, waving.

The Emperor watched the heavens another minute and then said, "Call him down to me."

"Ho, come down, come down! The Emperor wishes to see you!" called the servant, hands cupped to his shouting mouth.

The Emperor glanced in all directions while the flying man soared down the morning wind. He saw a farmer, early in his fields, watching the sky, and he noted where the farmer stood.

The flying man alit with a rustle of paper and a creak of bamboo reeds. He came proudly to the Emperor, clumsy in his rig, at last bowing before the old man.

"What have you done?" demanded the Emperor.

"I have flown in the sky, Your Excellency," replied the man.

"What *have* you done?" said the Emperor again.

"I have just told you!" cried the flier.

"You have told me nothing at all." The Emperor reached out a thin hand to touch the pretty paper and the birdlike keel of the apparatus. It smelled cool, of the wind.

"Is it not beautiful, Excellency?"

"Yes, too beautiful."

"It is the only one in the world!" smiled the man. "And I am the inventor."

"The *only* one in the world?"

"I swear it!"

"Who else knows of this?"

"No one. Not even my wife, who would think me mad with the sun. She thought I was making a kite. I rose in the night and walked to the cliffs far away. And when the morning breezes blew and the sun rose, I gathered my courage, Excellency, and leaped from the cliff. I flew! But my wife does not know of it."

"Well for her, then," said the Emperor. "Come along."

They walked back to the great house. The sun was full in the sky now, and the smell of the grass was refreshing. The Emperor, the servant, and the flier paused within the huge garden.

The Emperor clapped his hands. "Ho, guards!"

The guards came running.

"Hold this man."

The guards seized the flier.

"Call the executioner," said the Emperor.

"What's this!" cried the flier, bewildered. "What have I done?" He began to weep, so that the beautiful paper machine rustled.

"Here is the man who has made a certain machine," said the Emperor, "and yet asks us what he has created. He does not know himself. It is only necessary that he create, without knowing why he has done so, or what this thing will do."

The executioner came running with a sharp silver ax. He stood with his naked, large-muscled arms ready, his face covered with a serene white mask.

"One moment," said the Emperor. He turned to a nearby table upon which sat a machine that he himself had created. The Emperor took a tiny golden key from his own neck. He fitted this key to the tiny, delicate machine and wound it up. Then he set the machine going.

The machine was a garden of metal and jewels. Set in motion, birds sang in tiny metal trees, wolves walked through miniature forests, and tiny people ran in and out of sun and shadow, fanning themselves with miniature fans, listening to the tiny emerald birds, and standing by impossibly small but tinkling fountains.

"Is *it* not beautiful?" said the Emperor. "If you asked me what I have done here, I could answer you well. I have made birds sing, I have made forests murmur, I have set people to walking in this woodland, enjoying the leaves and shadows and songs. That is what I have done."

"But oh, Emperor!" pleaded the flier, on his knees, the tears pouring down his face. "I have done a similar thing! I have found beauty. I have flown on the morning wind. I have looked down on all the sleeping houses and gardens. I have smelled the sea and even *seen* it, beyond the hills, from my high place. And I have soared like a bird; oh, I cannot say how beautiful it is up there, in the sky, with the wind about me, the wind blowing me here like a feather, there like a fan, the way the sky smells in the morning! And how free one feels! *That* is beautiful, Emperor, that is beautiful too!"

"Yes," said the Emperor sadly, "I know it must be true. For I felt my heart move with you in the air and I wondered: What is it like? How does it feel? How do the distant pools look from so high? And how my houses and servants? Like ants? And how the distant towns not yet awake?"

"Then spare me!"

"But there are times," said the Emperor, more sadly still, "when one must lose a little beauty if one is to keep what little beauty one already has. I do not fear you, yourself, but I fear another man."

"What man?"

"Some other man who, seeing you, will build a thing of bright papers and bamboo like this. But the other man will have an evil face and an evil heart, and the beauty will be gone. It is this man I fear."

"Why? Why?"

"Who is to say that some day just such a man, in just such an apparatus of paper and reed, might not fly in the sky and drop huge stones upon the Great Wall of China?" said the Emperor.

No one moved or said a word.

"Off with his head," said the Emperor.

The executioner whirled his silver ax.

"Burn the kite and the inventor's body and bury their ashes together," said the Emperor.

The servants retreated to obey.

The Emperor turned to his hand-servant, who had seen the man flying. "Hold your tongue. It was all a dream, a most sorrowful and beautiful dream. And that farmer in the distant field who also saw, tell him it would pay him to consider it only a vision. If ever the word passes around, you and the farmer die within the hour."

"You are merciful, Emperor."

"No, not merciful," said the old man. Beyond the garden walls he saw the guards burning the beautiful machine of paper and reeds that smelled of the morning wind. He saw the dark smoke climb into the sky. "No, only very much bewildered and afraid." He saw the guards digging a tiny pit wherein to bury the ashes. "What is the life of one man against those of a million others? I must take solace from that thought."

He took the key from its chain about his neck and once more wound up the beautiful miniature garden. He stood looking out across the land at the Great Wall, the peaceful town, the green fields, the rivers and streams. He sighed. The tiny garden whirred its hidden and delicate machinery and set itself in motion; tiny people walked in forests, tiny foxes loped through sun-speckled glades in beautiful shining pelts, and among the tiny trees flew little bits of high song and bright blue and yellow colour, flying, flying, flying in that small sky.

"Oh," said the Emperor, closing his eyes, "look at the birds, look at the birds!"

RESPONSE

1. What choices does the Emperor Yuan have concerning the fate of the man who flies?

2. Determine why and how Emperor Yuan makes the choice that he does.

3. Respond to the question posed in the story, "What is the life of one man against those of a million others?"

EXTENSION

4. In small groups, discuss what you would have done in Emperor Yuan's place.

Trade the World Debt Crisis for Ecological Preservation

Tom Falvey

> Why is the tropical rain forest so important to life on this planet?
>
> What forces endanger the rain forest?

The living green belt of rain forest circling the Earth's equator is perhaps our single most valuable terrestrial asset. It is home to more species than any other ecosystem, and perhaps even all others combined: it is the planetary gene pool from which humanity itself emerged. It decisively regulates world climatic patterns, and forms the watershed protecting continental areas from becoming barren deserts.

A generation from now, in the rapidly emerging bio-technical era, the genetic resources of the rain forest will almost certainly be one of the most valuable resources on Earth—if they are not thoughtlessly squandered for an ephemeral profit now.

Yet, tropical rain forests, teeming with life in their natural state, are permanently sterilized by human exploitation. Their fertility is locked into the forest canopy itself rather than stored in the soil as in temperate zones. Once the forest is cleared, the blazing sun and torrential rains rapidly leach and bake the land into a barren desert or scrub zone. This is happening with frightening speed throughout the tropical world.

Impoverished tropical nations must be given a practical economic incentive to preserve this global life-support system. This could be found in a resolution of the world debt crises through a settlement of accounts that factors in the nonrenewable global habitat as value offsetting the paper value of monetary debt. This could be accomplished by Third World nations placing their virgin tropical rain forest lands in a United Nations trust or World Park as the common heritage of all humankind—in return for the cancellation of all foreign debt.

Obviously such a plan could benefit the Third World by relieving it of the crushing, and ultimately explosive, burden of foreign debt—and by protecting their lands from the humanly catalyzed process of desertification that has already ruined much of Africa. But what of its impact upon the banks and governments to whom these debts are due? Would not such a utopian scheme cause economic chaos and institutional collapse in the developed world?

First, we must realize the inevitability of an eventual default in any case. These massive debts simply cannot and will not be paid, and any adverse change in the world economic situation will put that open secret under the spotlight. This proposal at least permits us to save tangible natural assets and nail down long-term ecological stability in return for retiring worthless paper.

Third World nations owe the banks and governments of the developed world approximately $1 trillion. This is less than the cost of the Reagan administration's $1.5 trillion 1981-87 defence buildup, and a mere fraction of the contemplated but highly uncertain Star Wars programme. Surely if we can sink so much money into unproductive military assets, we can find a rational way to absorb this much smaller cost for the long-term defence of our planet against certain environmental disaster.

Indeed, from a national security viewpoint, this proposal has many benefits. By the turn of the century we are far more likely to be threatened by chaos in desertified, environmentally ravaged Third World nations, embittered by the despoilation of their natural resources to feed the West's wasteful consumerism, than by the unlikely prospect of war between the superpowers.

Implementation of this proposal would not only preserve these resources and environments, it would also have important political spin-offs both in terms of international co-operation and of encouraging long-term rationality in policymaking. And we should not ignore the intangible values: a global tropical forest preserve would be a sanity buffer in an overpopulated world, a refuge for the human spirit as well as for endangered species.

Sensible as it is, there is still no doubt that implementation of this proposal would have a profound economic impact on the financial institutions and general economies of the developed world. Change, though always resisted, is not always bad. In fact, major adjustments are needed to adapt to profound structural changes in the world economy and to correct the unsustainable domestic behaviour of the lender nations.

The steady flow of interest payments has masked an underlying shift in economic reality generated by a trillion dollar investment in Third World economies since the early 1970's. Some of that money has been wasted, more has been stolen—but much of it has been sunk into infrastructure, productive capacity, and resource development. That growth, and evolutionary change in the global economy, have reached the point where the system must "moult": throw off its old structural shell and formalize a new structure adequate to the current situation.

For lender nations, especially the United States, which has been living far beyond its means in the expectation that the world owes it an indefinite continuation of the comfortable patterns of the past, a controlled default will entail internal domestic changes. But this is better seen not as a tragedy but as an opportunity to reconstitute our financial systems with an altered set of investment priorities conducive to more balanced and sustainable economies.

That we are now so alienated from our essential nature that we will poison the inheritance of our offspring to indulge a grotesquely wasteful consumerism is a profound indictment of the current system. So too is its insistence on endless growth: "growth for the sake of growth is the ideology of the cancer cell." Why should we blindly perpetuate the institutions that have made such a mess of things and now cannot even survive in their own narrowly defined monetary terms?

Changes in the real economy are necessary, overdue, and consistent with existing values. The only real obstacles to them are political rather than technical. They would undercut the vested interests of bloated financial institutions and their dinosaur corporate progeny—but these have already failed in their own frame of reference, which is why we have both a world and a domestic debt crisis in the first place.

This debt crisis is going to come to a head someday: we can either bury our heads in the sand and wait for an explosive political/military confrontation—or we can rationally negotiate and plan a positive adjustment of both the global and domestic economies. Certainly the U.S. government has been planning for a debt default at least since this crisis became public in August 1982. Why not institute a controlled release of this tension in a positive direction rather than waiting for it to blow up in our faces?

By cashing in worthless international debt in return for preserving the world's tropical rain forest we accomplish three goals:

- We would save a vital planetary asset, the most important climatic regulator and gene pool on Earth. In the eyes of future generations—for eons to come, not merely our children and great grandchildren—no other consideration even comes close to this.
- It would relieve misery-ridden Third World economies of an unbearable and politically intolerable burden. Such a move at this time would be a significant catalyst to the fragile democracies that have recently emerged in Latin America and elsewhere.
- It would provide an honorable rationale to clean up many domestic structural problems in the United Nations, opening up to the decentralized, job producing, energy and resource saving measures most people realize are eventually necessary.

We could all get on with the Millennium, having unshackled our own and the world economy from the debts of the past, and having locked in the living environmental guarantee of the future.

RESPONSE

1. In one sentence, summarize Falvey's proposed solution to the world debt crisis.
2. Explain the benefits of Falvey's proposal.
3. What do you think are the major drawbacks to Falvey's proposed solution?
4. Do you agree with Falvey's assertions about "wasteful consumerism" and "endless growth"? Explain.

EXTENSION

5. In a small group, attempt to develop a practical plan to solve one of: the world debt; the destruction of the rain forest; endless growth; uncontrolled consumerism.
6. With a partner or in a small group, research a recent, successful ecological endeavour and present your findings to the class.

Blessed Are the Peacemakers

The Very Reverend Lois M. Wilson

> In your own words define *peace*; define *security*.
>
> Is it possible to have one without the other?

Threats to Survival

We are now living in the dark shadow of an arms race more intense, and of systems of injustice more widespread, more dangerous and more costly, than the world has ever known. Never before has the human race been so close to total self-destruction. After August 6, 1945, the threat to the world's survival became qualitatively different from anything known before in human history. In an incredibly short time, humankind moved from the horrors of Hiroshima and Nagasaki to the likelihood—unless we act courageously—that life on the whole planet will be totally devastated. A moment of madness, a miscalculated strategic adventure, a chance combination of computer errors, a misperception of the other's intention, an honest mistake—any one of the foregoing could set off a nuclear holocaust. And even in the absence of declared war, nuclear weapons claim victims through nuclear weapons testing and the dumping of nuclear wastes. Is it any wonder, then, that so many have committed themselves to working for human survival by focusing their attention and priorities on stopping the arms race?

Yet for millions in the Third World, on whatever continent they live, the most immediate threat to survival is not posed by nuclear or conventional weapons. A nuclear war is not required for thousands to perish daily, in nations both rich and poor, because of hunger and starvation. Human misery and suffering have reached unprecedented levels. Conflicts between East and West and between North and South intersect in the Third World to cause massive injustice, homelessness, starvation and death for many, as well as oppression and despair. Millions are left homeless, expelled from their native lands as refugees or exiles, as wave after wave of agony sweeps over the world. Is it any wonder, then, that so many have committed themselves to working for human survival by focusing their attention and priorities on food and clean water in the Third World? And so Barbara Ward said, "I would put clean water at the very forefront of the possibility of getting a stable world in the next thirty years."

Different Interpretations of Security and Peace

Some people feel that peace can be secured and maintained through a system of threats. Security, they believe, lies in deterrence, and in always having weapons superior to those of the enemy. Defined as the primary objective, security must be achieved by any and every means. Sometimes this definition is applied to *national* security; then, any new military strategies and increases in military spending are justified because they lead to greater "national security." National security becomes an all-consuming goal.

Other people feel that peace can be secured and maintained only through the creation of a just, participatory and sustainable society. They speak more often of collective security than of national security. Their priority is not more money for arms, but food for their children and clean water for their villages. They would claim that only by sharing the world's resources in a more equitable and just way, on a sustained basis, can security be offered to all. Security, they believe, is the product of a social, political and spiritual environment, based on love and justice, which serves the welfare and security of all. Ultimately, we must see the true security of individuals and nations as the consequence of global justice.

Let me remind you at this point of a statement made by the World Council of Churches when it met in Vancouver in 1983.

The arms trade is a new form of intervention maintaining and developing dominance/dependence relationships and encouraging repression and violation of human rights. Militarism leads to massive allocation of human and material resources to research and production in the military sector of all countries at the cost of lowering the priority of meeting the needs of human development. We believe the time has come when the churches must unequivocally declare that the production, deployment and the use of nuclear weapons are a crime against humanity, and such activities must be condemned on ethical and theological grounds.

These differences in interpretations of peace and security are not new. One of the first conferences on disarmament was held at the Hague in 1907. But what is significant is what happened *around* that conference. Korea had sent a representative to plead Korean independence from Japan. But Britain, France and America (in alliance with Japan) refused the Korean plan for independence and self-development. The consequent suicide of the Korean delegate in a hotel in the Hague demonstrated to the world the anguish of a colonially-exploited people.

One person who continued in the tradition of understanding that there is no peace unless one has rice to eat and a roof over one's head, was Dietrich Bonhoeffer, later martyred under the Nazi regime. Speaking at a peace conference in 1935 in Denmark, out of the German context of that time, he maintained that there is no path to peace through armed security, but only through just and equitable economic and social relationships. His speech did not please those who attended.

Effects of the Arms Race on the Third World

The attention given to the arms race by the developed countries has grossly distorted their economic and social priorities and put an enormous drain on their finite resources; both of these developments have had a major effect on the Third World. The arms race is now predominantly a race in modern technology. Weapons research is driven by the pursuit of a final technological solution to the goal of security. Weapon improvements have led to new military strategies and have dramatically increased the probability of nuclear war.

Moreover, military research has grown more and more beyond political control. The massive allocation of human and material resources to military research and development (fifty percent of all natural scientists work directly or indirectly for military purposes) has distorted the developed world's perception of what is socially useful and necessary. Very little scientific or technological inventiveness is concentrated on disarmament or development: many electronic gadgets that we use in every day life (such as pocket calculators) are offshoots of military research; yet, no safe and reliable technological method of birth control for women has yet been developed.

The growing gap between the rich and the poor, exacerbated by the cost of the arms race, alienates the poor and hungry even more, and robs them of any hope of survival. UNICEF stresses the need for a "revolution in child survival to improve the state of the world's children." And I want to emphasize that what is happening to children is *abominable*. They are *sinned against*. But it is the mothers of these children who are the key to change. In relation to hunger, the essential role of women is rarely recognized. In Africa, women do between sixty and eighty percent of all agricultural work. They bear the children, carry the water, produce the food and gather the fuel. It should then be obvious why people become intensely angry when resources legitimately expected to be used to train and support these women are instead used by industrialized countries to continue to dominate the world and preserve their prerogatives of power through escalating arms production.

There is a growing anger among the poor of this planet. They are angry because we of the industrialized nations are not angry enough. They are angry because producing arms to fuel the conflict between East and West takes precedence over their profound needs for basic human necessities. And unless global priorities are changed, that growing anger will develop into a major threat to peace and security for the whole world. Already at a crucial point, the escalating arms race deepens the social and economic crises in the Third World. By imposing unbelievably heavy debts on the Third World to support trade for industrialized countries; by militarizing space, which results in a scarcity of resources for the Third World; by developing military technology rather than appropriate technology for a hungry world; and by supporting a war culture based on violence (which concentrates its power through political, economic and military might), the developed world denies human beings in the Third World the legitimate aspiration of a peaceful, prosperous future.

The Roots of Violence

A desire to grab and maintain economic advantage is at the roots of the use of violence. Certainly, the expansion of trade and the growth of the developed countries' standards of living would have been impossible without the raw materials from the colonies and dependent nations. The history of colonialism is a history of world expansionism, colonial exploitation, slavery and the grabbing of land and resources.

I'll never forget my first visit to Westminster Abbey in London. I had been taught that it was a wonderful place; but most of it was statues of people who had slaughtered other people in this war or that war. History for me in school was a series of dates of wars. It was the history of violence that we were taught. And until we recover our whole history as human beings, including our history of peaceful co-operation, all of our rhetoric is going to be in vain.

Present militaristic efforts to "defend our way of life" (i.e., our place in the global hierarchy) are in reality aimed at maintaining the status quo, which is arranged in favour of the industrialized countries. They exploit cheap labour in Third World countries; they keep the prices cheap for raw materials by establishing prices through the creditor's club; they give tax-free incentives to those doing business in Third World countries; they assure themselves access to fuel and markets upon which their economic prosperity depends; and they support military dictatorships to keep the lid on it all politically. Because investment is simply not profitable in an unstable environment, repression and human rights violations usually accompany efforts to keep a politically unstable situation on an even keel.

Since World War II, there has been a frightening international-ization of wealth and power. Five hundred companies account for from eighty to ninety percent of international trade. Important lobbies are created by transnational corporations to maximize unfettered free trade and to take profits whenever they can. Power and wealth have interpenetrated the world like a cancer. And so the power elites have made the militarization of Third World societies a priority, in order to maintain the stability that investment requires.

Usually the media is also used as a tool for social control, both to promote consumerism and to mesmerize unsophisticated people into social apathy. I recall a visit made to one of the desperate slums on the outskirts of Santiago, Chile. Those same slum dwellers who had not enough calcium in their diet to retain their teeth gathered to watch the community television promote electric toothbrushes for all. Later, we watched Dallas and the Flintstones with dubbed Spanish sound tracks: bread and circuses to assist the military in keeping an ordered society! I have seen small clumps of people in Third World countries watching television, and they *know* how we live. There is a growing anger among the poor on this planet, and that growing anger will escalate and continue to be a major threat to peace and security unless the global priorities are changed.

According to the Canadian Churches' Task Force on Corporate Responsibility, the price the Ford Motor Company paid for the privilege of operating in South Africa was to sign an agreement with the South African government to support the military forces protecting the status quo (i.e., pro-apartheid) in case of a black uprising. Ford signed a contract with the South African police and military to supply vehicles in case of an emergency and to allow weapons to be stored on its premises in case the military needed them suddenly. For all of this, Ford would receive a tax deduction as part of "normal operating expenses." When I questioned the president of Ford about signing such an agreement, he answered, "But we had no choice." The translation of this is: "Support of the military in South Africa was the price we were willing to pay to protect our lucrative investments and support our way of life." All of this, and more, goes on.

Canadians are only dimly aware of the connections between militarism, the build-up of arms on a global scale and the poverty and oppression of the Third World. While militarism continues unchecked throughout the world, the deprivation of hundreds of millions of people in the Third World increases. A direct connection between militarism and deprivation lies in the arms trade. Canadian military exports to the Third World now amount to about $150 million a year. It would be a step forward if Canada were to place the neglected issue of the arms trade on the international agenda, and show its support for curtailing the arms trade by supplying its own detailed statistics to an international arms trade register. Then we would begin to be aware of the extent of the arms trade and who Canada's customers are.

The Cost of the Arms Race to a Stable Global Development

The world spends the equivalent of nearly U.S. $2 billion each day for armaments. This does not include the enormous projected costs of developing the Strategic Defense Initiative (SDI). The disparity between defence expenditures on the one hand and expenditures on behalf of a stable global development on the other are so wide that it boggles the mind. The real dimensions of the coming peace and security crisis include vital issues relating to population, environment, and the economy.

Population. By the year 2000, the world's population will be six billion. It continues to double every thirty years. The growing population will mean greater competition for scarce world resources. Growing poverty will increase the likelihood of unrest and war, adding to the chances that the superpowers themselves may become militarily entangled in an effort to protect their economic interests. But the greatest crisis in population growth is the toll on the earth's resources and life support systems. Billions of people will have to struggle just to get enough resources to stay alive.

Environment. During the past four decades, half of the world's forests have been felled. By the year 2000, half of what remains will be gone. Tropical rain forests will have disappeared, although they are the lungs of the earth. At least ten thousand tons of radio-active waste is awaiting disposal—somewhere. (People of the Pacific tell the rest of the world: "Bury it in your own backyard, if it's so safe.")

The Economy. And then there are the hopeless debts that the countries of the South owe the banks of the North—about U.S. $800 billion—with little hope of repayment. There is a decided reluctance on the part of the creditor nations even to sit down around the table with the debtors to re-schedule the debts. Yet common sense and equity require that developing countries be helped, not penalized further, when they are buffeted by economic shocks completely beyond their control. Rich nations must make concessions. There is an immediate need to re-evaluate the debts, to limit interest rates and lengthen repayment periods, or possibly to cancel debts outright for the least developed countries. There is an urgent need to co-operate with and strengthen United Nations institutions in order to create a new international economic order. There is a pressing need to restructure the international financial system according to the principles of universality, equitable representation, accountability and fair reward for labour.

An Integrated Approach

We desperately need to reverse the trend toward disintegration and disorder in the multilateral trade and financial systems on which the world depends for survival and prosperity. Solutions will require an integrated, co-operative, global approach. Developed countries, for example, will find it hard to enforce pollution controls if industries simply move their operations to countries where controls are nonexistent. And Third World countries are unlikely to make pollution controls a priority in the face of their most pressing problems of poverty and debt repayment.

The Other Costs

We are accustomed to thinking about the costs of the arms race in terms of military spending alone. That is, annually, about $10 billion for Canada, and about $1 trillion for the world. But we need to be equally aware of the other costs:
1. International institutions, because of our inability to renew or reform them, have been paralyzed by the military build-up and lack of trust between countries.
2. The entire globe faces environmental dangers and damage because the arms race has taken precedence over ecology.
3. The people of many countries have suffered privations because their governments have spent more money on arms imports than on food imports.
4. The world's economy has suffered structural damage as a consequence of the war system.
5. National policies exist which fail to reflect the link between disarmament and development.

The Role of a Person of Conscience

As citizens of Canada, we should support these policies through the political processes available to us:
1. The long held goal of 0.7% of GNP for development assistance should be retargeted for 1990 rather than delayed until 1995 and be focused more clearly on helping deprived people to meet their own basic needs, including food, clean water, health, education and employment.
2. This expenditure should no longer be tied to items of Canadian origin, so as to permit tenders from developing countries and, in due course, allow for general international competitive tenders.
3. Canadian government funds should not be used, directly or indirectly, in association with export credits to secure capital contracts for Canadian firms. It is shabby to present as *aid* funds

which are spent in promotion of Canadian exports in *trade*. Export subsidization and development assistance are not the same thing. The "Aid-Trade Fund" should be removed from the official development assistance account.

4. Food aid should be employed only for emergency relief. Its use in other areas is fraught with dangers, particularly when it competes with local production.

In addition to supporting the above policies, we should read widely from the literature, poems, songs and expressions of despair and agony that come out of the Third World. "Songs of the Unsung" from a Malaysian poet speak of unpoetic subjects like war, poverty and hunger. We should subscribe to magazines and publications coming directly out of the life of the common people of Asia, Africa, Latin America.

We need to be conscious of being part of the larger peace movement in the world. The particular issue we are working on is connected to many global issues in this interdependent world. We should turn our backs on isolationism.

We should challenge the violence in our own culture by choosing creative alternatives. Bear in mind that the essence of being human is to take part in caring human relationships. This is not optional for a human being. Caring for another and for the whole of creation is what defines us as human beings.

We must remember that every utterance of faith in weapons of mass destruction—every justification of violence and oppression—is a litany of death. Every unjust law, every untimely death, every use of human talent to create more weapons is a litany of death and contrary to God's purpose in creation. So sing a litany of life. Blessed are the peacemakers.

RESPONSE

1. By citing specific examples from current world affairs, show how "Conflicts between East and West and between North and South intersect in the Third World. . . ."

2. How does your understanding of peace and security compare with Wilson's understanding as presented in the essay?

3. Summarize the author's description of women and children in the Third World.

4. Describe the behaviour of a person you know whom Wilson would term a "person of conscience."

EXTENSION

5. As a class, compile a list of peacemaking activities that you could employ in your home and school environments. Choose a single course of action and implement it.

Our Backs Against the Bomb, Our Eyes on the Stars

Rusty Schweickart

> Why are national borders established?
>
> How are these borders established and maintained?

An astronaut suspended between earth and moon, Archibald MacLeish wrote, sees the earth "as it truly is, small and blue and beautiful in that eternal silence where it floats." Closer to home, there's another revelation that comes from circling this planet. As you pass from sunlight into darkness and back again every hour and a half, you become startlingly aware how artificial are the thousands of boundaries we've created to separate and define. And for the first time in your life you feel in your gut the precious unity of the earth and all the living things it supports. The dissonance between this unity you see and the separateness of human groupings that you know exists is starkly apparent.

During my space flight, I came to appreciate my profound connection to the home planet and the process of life evolving in our special corner of the universe, and I grasped that I was part of a vast and mysterious dance whose outcome will be determined largely by human values and actions.

As I floated outside Apollo 9 with sunlight streaming past me, streaking over the Pacific at 17,000 miles an hour, I realized I was there on behalf of all humanity, that it was my responsibility to communicate this experience to my fellow beings, perhaps give them a glimmering of what I saw, what impressed itself upon me.

It's more than a metaphor to say we're children of the stars. The elements that form our bodies were forged in stellar explosions eons ago, and have been combined and sculptured locally into DNA templates by the warm glow of our own docile star. We're amazing beings, who wonder about our origins and purpose, our past and future. Above all, we can think and do. We can wrestle with ethical dilemma, ambiguity, and paradox. By any measure, we're a marvelous experiment.

But we're now also capable of terminating this cosmic experiment. The decision to unleash the devastation of the atom appears to depend on the whims of only two men, but in fact many others are involved: other heads of state, generals, faceless terrorists, even an errant computer. Any one could trigger events that would lead to hundreds of millions of deaths, if not planetary extinction.

Is anybody actually in charge? Or have we lost the handle on our technology? It sometimes seems as if our machines have developed a life of their own.

But like it or not, we're married to our tools. And while we must wrestle with ourselves over how to control them, we have no choice but to make them. By nature, we're toolmakers, tool users. We see limitless possibilities for organizing and concentrating material and energy to extend our capabilities and to ease the burdens of life. Our tools also include weapons, which are sometimes used for protection, at other times to coerce and kill.

This marriage of human and machine has created the ultimate predicament. Our technology has progressed to where we can now manipulate energy and material to free ourselves from our earthly womb, or to destroy all life on it. Which will it be? I believe the right choice can only be made if we overcome our fears, our distrust of each other, our assumption of separateness.

Our future—indeed, our survival—is closely tied to the idea of our *common* destiny, and we must act, individually and together, out of an appreciation of that grand vision.

The extent of popular support for going into space always amazes me. Rich or poor, educated or illiterate, male or female, young or old, all over the world people are intrigued by and dedicated to the exploration of space. We've always been fascinated by the stars, planets, and celestial phenomena. Who among us isn't awed by the heavenly display on a starry night? Who hasn't pondered his or her place in the universe beneath clear skies in a mountain valley or on the high desert?

I don't know why this feeling is so common, but I suspect it's embedded within our nature. It seems to me that as we approach the day when life moves outward from the earth, realizing our ancient dreams, this yearning becomes a collective act, an extension of the will of all life to grow beyond our planetary womb. It's almost as if we're groping toward the stars.

I call this cosmic birth. Like human birth, it's a consequence of the nature of life, and extends the evolutionary path into the cosmic arena. I also believe that, like the human model, it moves us from a one-way relationship of dependency to a two-way relationship of love and responsibility.

It's in this context that I think we must act in order to ensure the continuation of the life experiment. But how? Will our cosmic birth buy bread for the Third World? Settle disputes in the Middle East?

Action, for good or ill, comes out of vision. What I've been talking about is envisioning our role in life, in the cosmos. When I understand you and me to be one, I think and act differently from when I see us as separate. Yet while we may see ourselves as members of a community, there's no escaping individual responsibility. History emerges from a succession of individual, apparently independent, actions.

I've often thought of an experience I had as being symbolic of the human dilemma. Many years ago I was a 24-year-old fighter pilot stationed in the Philippines. I was assigned to an F-100 squadron, and every fourth week or so it would be my turn to stand nuclear alert at an airbase on Taiwan. We had four planes there, parked at the end of the runway, fully fueled, a nuclear weapon slung underneath each, prepared to go at a moment's notice.

We pilots would lounge inside the alert shack, playing cards or reading or sleeping, waiting for the red phone to ring—and hoping it never would. The phone sat there, ready to spring to life at any second, and we sat there, prepared to leap into the air with our weapons. That wasn't something you thought about constantly; you spent too many hours doing nothing except getting used to your situation. But the reality was always lurking just below the surface.

About once a week each of the planes would have to be exchanged for a fresh one. The bombs were very patient, as it were, but the planes would begin leaking hydraulic fluid after a week or so if they weren't exercised. Whenever this happened, the pilot who was assigned to that plane would be notified and he would strap on his sidearm and go out to the ramp to monitor the operation. The ground crews would roll a cradle under the nuclear weapon; it would be lowered from the plane, wheeled off to the side, and the flight crew would tow away the old leaker, move in a fresh plane, and reload the weapon. The whole operation took twenty or thirty minutes, and while the planes were being shuttled in and out, the bomb would just sit there off to the side waiting patiently. This process was always done at night—in order, I suppose, to minimize the number of unwanted eyes watching it.

The pilot had nothing particular to do during the procedure. He was there just to watch, since it would be his plane to fly if the red phone rang. The crews knew what they were doing, and so whenever it was my turn to go through this drill, I would watch until they moved the bomb off to the side, and then I would climb on top of it and lie there, looking up at the stars.

As I did, I would imagine, step by step, the role I might be called on to play. I did this with as much realism as I could because I knew that if the phone rang I wouldn't have time to think about it. I would imagine hearing the phone ring, listening to the voice on the other end reading the code words, verifying them with those in the envelope I carried, throwing on my G suit and flight jacket, and running out the door to my plane. If I visualized this well, my heart would begin to race, as it would no doubt have done in reality. I would then imagine myself starting the engine, taking off, and turning onto the course that would take me toward my target on the mainland. Each of the checkpoints on the way were fixed in my mind and I would visualize passing over each of the towns and villages I had never seen, adjusting my speed and course slightly, until I was approaching my destination. Throttling up to maximum thrust I would imagine pulling up over the target until I was at that exact point where I would release the bomb.

Would I do it? That was the question I wanted to face; that was the purpose of the terrifying ritual I would go through, trying to face the reality of why I was there, and what my responsibility might be. Up until that moment in the mission, everything was more or less automatic. I was a good pilot and I had no doubt I would end up over the target with my finger on the button, facing that ultimate decision. I would hang there in my mind's eye, stopping time, wrestling with the question "On what basis do I decide whether or not to release this nuclear weapon, knowing that hundreds of thousands of people would die as a result?" (The military targets were often close to population centers.)

My back pressed against the bomb, I would look at the stars

and search my soul (and the heavens as well) for the moral basis on which I might decide. I was aware of the individual moral burden of an action that would kill people I would never see. And I was also aware of the complex system of which I was a part, a system whose purpose of preventing war through deterrence would be corrupted (and the world therefore endangered) should the possibility of my electing not to release the weapon be known. I knew I'd have very little knowledge, if any, of what was going on in the rest of the world. Was half of it already gone? What about my family? My home town? I wouldn't know their fate.

Even so, did these questions have any relevance to the decision I had to make? How can societies function if, in the most critical situations, individuals claim for themselves the right to decide that which has already been decided by society as a whole? I knew personally the people two levels up the line leading to the red phone. They were good, responsible people. And I was sure this was true all the way up to the President. My responsibility as an officer was to execute orders passed down by those above me, who, I felt, were as morally sensitive as I was.

Each time I'd go through the ritual I would force myself to decide anew what my decision would be. Each time I concluded I would drop the bomb.

Years later I found myself in positions of power within government, where my decisions dramatically affected the lives of many people. These weren't decisions of war and peace, but they often required a rapid response and, moreover, were often irrevocable. As I watched myself at this upper end of the decision-making process, I realized with horror the poor quality and incompleteness of the information on which I had to base such decisions. I even sensed an inverse correlation between the decisions that were most ethically challenging and/or time-critical and the quality of the information upon which I had to act. I began to understand how much human frailty and subjectivity were woven into the most critical decision making.

And after much agony I came to realize, knowing what I know now, that if I had to decide again, lying there under the stars, my back pressed against the bomb, I wouldn't drop it. My specific decision isn't the point—it's rather that as a young man I was unwilling to trust my own sense of rightness when facing a momentous moral dilemma. I now understand that we can't pass along such decisions to higher authority, for there is no higher authority than that which exists in each of us, individually, as we face our complicated and ambiguous world. In my view, it's these personal moral choices, when repeated and aggregated in the behaviour of families, of communities, of nations, that are the very essence of our survival.

So here we are, approaching the twenty-first century, our backs pressed against the bomb and our eyes on the stars. Our dilemma becomes increasingly daunting. Will our vision of the human future be large and clear enough to lift us beyond the uncertainties and fears of our cosmic birth? Will we have the wisdom and courage to accept the individual moral authority within each of us? Or will we defer to experts and impersonal systems of authority in the false belief that in them reside greater wisdom and morality? In how we answer these questions may lie the outcome of the great experiment of life.

RESPONSE

1. What insights about the planet and humanity are prompted by the author's space flight?

2. In what sense does the author imply that life is an experiment?

3. a) Do you agree with Schweickart's statement that "while we may see ourselves as members of a community, there's no escaping individual responsibility"?

   b) What realization compelled Schweickart to reverse his decision about dropping the bomb?

EXTENSION

4. "There is no higher authority than that which exists in each of us, individually . . . [in] these personal moral choices. . . ." List the specific ways in which your personal moral decisions can have an effect on the survival of humankind.

Canadians:
What Do They Want?

Margaret Atwood

What do you want Americans to know about Canada?

With reference to specific historical examples, develop a definition of imperialism.

Last month, during a poetry reading, I tried out a short prose poem called "How to Like Men." It began by suggesting that one start with the feet. Unfortunately, the question of jackboots soon arose, and things went on from there. After the reading I had a conversation with a young man who thought I had been unfair to men. He wanted men to be liked totally, not just from the heels to the knees, and not just as individuals but as a group; and he thought it negative and inegalitarian of me to have alluded to war and rape. I pointed out that as far as any of us knew these were two activities not widely engaged in by women, but he was still upset. "We're both in this together," he protested. I admitted that this was so; but could he, maybe, see that our relative positions might be a little different.

This is the conversation one has with Americans, even, uh, *good* Americans, when the dinner-table conversation veers round to Canadian-American relations. "We're in this together," they like to say, especially when it comes to continental energy reserves. How do you *explain* to them, as delicately as possible, why they are not categorically beloved? It gets like the old Lifebuoy ads: even their best friends won't tell them. And Canadians are supposed to be their best friends, right? Members of the family?

Well, sort of. Across the river from Michigan, so near and yet so far, there I was at the age of eight, reading *their* Donald Duck comic books (originated, however, by one of *ours*; yes, Walt Disney's parents were Canadian) and coming at the end to Popsicle Pete, who promised me the earth if only I would save wrappers, but took it all away from me again with a single asterisk: Offer Good Only in the United States. Some cynical members of the world community may be forgiven for thinking that the same asterisk is there, in invisible ink, on the Constitution and the Bill of Rights.

But quibbles like that aside, and good will assumed, how does one go about liking Americans? Where does one begin? Or, to put it another way, why did the Canadian women lock themselves in the john during a '70s "international" feminist conference being held in Toronto? Because the American sisters were being "imperialist," that's why.

But then, it's always a little naive of Canadians to expect that Americans, of whatever political stamp, should stop being imperious. How can they? The fact is that the United States is an empire and Canada is to it as Gaul was to Rome.

It's hard to explain to Americans what it feels like to be a Canadian. Pessimists among us would say that one has to translate the experience into their own terms and that this is necessary because Americans are incapable of thinking in any other terms— and this in itself is part of the problem. (Witness all those draft dodgers who went into culture shock when they discovered to their horror that Toronto was not Syracuse.)

Here is a translation: Picture a Mexico with a population ten times larger than that of the United States. That would put it at about two billion. Now suppose that the official American language is Spanish, that 75 percent of the books Americans buy and 90 percent of the movies they see are Mexican, and that the profits flow across the border to Mexico. If an American does scrape it together to make a movie, the Mexicans won't let him show it in the States, because they own the distribution outlets. If anyone tries to change this ratio, not only the Mexicans but many fellow Americans cry "National chauvinism," or, even more effectively, "National socialism." After all, the American public prefers the Mexican product. It's what they're used to.

Retranslate and you have the current American-Canadian picture. It's changed a little recently, not only on the cultural front. For instance, Canada, some think a trifle late, is attempting to regain control of its own petroleum industry. Americans are predictably angry. They think of Canadian oil as *theirs*.

"What's mine is yours," they have said for years, meaning

exports; "What's yours is mine" means ownership and profits. Canadians are supposed to do retail buying, not controlling, or what's an empire for? One could always refer Americans to history, particularly that of their own revolution. They objected to the colonial situation when they themselves were a colony; but then, revolution is considered one of a very few home-grown American products that definitely are not for export.

Objectively, one cannot become too self-righteous about this state of affairs. Canadians owned lots of things, including their souls, before World War II. After that they sold, some say because they had put too much into financing the war, which created a capital vacuum (a position they would not have been forced into if the Americans hadn't kept out of the fighting for so long, say the sore losers). But for whatever reason, capital flowed across the border in the '50s, and Canadians, traditionally sock-under-the-mattress hoarders, were reluctant to invest in their own country. Americans did it for them and ended up with a large part of it, which they retain to this day. In every sellout there's a seller as well as a buyer, and the Canadians did a thorough job of trading their birthright for a mess.

That's on the capitalist end, but when you turn to the trade union side of things you find much the same story, except that the sellout happened in the '30s under the banner of the United Front. Now Canadian workers are finding that in any empire the colonial branch plants are the first to close, and what could be a truly progressive labor movement has been weakened by compromised bargains made in international union headquarters south of the border.

Canadians are sometimes snippy to Americans at cocktail parties. They don't like to feel owned and they don't like having been sold. But what really bothers them—and it's at this point that the United States and Rome part company—is the wide-eyed innocence with which their snippiness is greeted.

Innocence becomes ignorance when seen in the light of international affairs, and though ignorance is one of the spoils of conquest—the Gauls always knew more about the Romans than the Romans knew about them—the world can no longer afford America's ignorance. Its ignorance of Canada, though it makes Canadians bristle, is a minor and relatively harmless example. More dangerous is the fact that individual Americans seem not to know that the United States is an imperial power and is behaving like one. They don't want to admit that empires dominate, invade and subjugate—and live on the proceeds—or, if they do admit it, they believe in their divine right to do so. The export of divine right is much more harmful than the export of Coca-Cola, though they may turn out to be much the same thing in the end.

Other empires have behaved similarly (the British somewhat better, Genghis Khan decidedly worse); but they have not expected to be *liked* for it. It's the final Americanism, this passion for being liked. Alas, many Americans are indeed likable; they are often more generous, more welcoming, more enthusiastic, less picky and sardonic than Canadians, and it's not enough to say it's only because they can afford it. Some of that revolutionary spirit still remains: the optimism, the 18th-century belief in the fixability of almost anything, the conviction of the possibility of change. However, at cocktail parties and elsewhere one must be able to tell the difference between an individual and a foreign policy. Canadians can no longer afford to think of Americans as only a spectator sport. If the President of the United States blows up the world, we will unfortunately be doing more than watching it on television. "No annihilation without representation" sounds good as a slogan, but if we run it up the flagpole, who's going to salute?

We *are* all in this together. For Canadians, the question is how to survive it. For Americans there is no question, because there does not have to be. Canada is just that vague, cold place where their uncle used to go fishing, before the lakes went dead from acid rain.

How do you like Americans? Individually, it's easier. Your average American is no more responsible for the state of affairs than your average man is for war and rape. Any Canadian who is so narrow-minded as to dislike Americans merely on principle is missing out on one of the good things in life. The same might be said, to women, of men. As a group, as a foreign policy, it's harder. But if you like men, you can like Americans. Cautiously. Selectively. Beginning with the feet. One at a time.

RESPONSE

1. According to Margaret Atwood, what are the most significant developments in Canadian-American relations since World War II?

2. Do you agree with Atwood that the U.S. acts as an imperial power towards Canada? Explain.

3. Reread the first and last paragraphs of the essay. Explain the correlation that Atwood draws between men and Americans. Do you agree with her opinion?

EXTENSION

4. In small groups, compile reports on various aspects of The Canada-U.S. Free Trade Agreement. Present your findings to the class. Speculate on the changes in Canadian-American relations as a result of this agreement.

5. Write a personal essay on an aspect of life in Canada that you feel is not for sale.

Aging

God Is Not a Fish Inspector

W. D. Valgardson

> In what ways do you think you will remain unchanged as you age?

Although Emma made no noise as she descended, Fusi Bergman knew his daughter was watching him from the bottom of the stairs.

"God will punish you," she promised in a low, intense voice.

"Render unto Caesar what is Caesar's," he snapped. "God's not a fish inspector. He doesn't work for the government."

By the light of the front ring of the kitchen stove, he had been drinking a cup of coffee mixed half and half with whisky. Now, he shifted in his captain's chair so as to partly face the stairs. Though he was unable to make out more than the white blur of Emma's nightgown, after living with her for 48 years he knew exactly how she would look if he turned on the light.

She was tall and big boned with the square, pugnacious face of a bulldog. Every inch of her head would be crammed with metal curlers and her angular body hidden by a plain white cotton shift that hung from her broad shoulders like a tent. Whenever she was angry with him, she always stood rigid and white lipped, her hands clenched at her sides.

"You prevaricate," she warned. "You will not be able to prevaricate at the gates of Heaven."

He drained his cup, sighed, and pulled on his jacket. As he opened the door, Fusi said, "He made fish to catch. There is no place in the Bible where it says you can't catch fish when you are threescore and ten."

"You'll be the ruin of us," she hissed as he closed the door on her.

She was aggressive and overbearing, but he knew her too well to be impressed. Behind her forcefulness, there was always that trace of self-pity nurtured in plain women who go unmarried until they think they have been passed by. Even if they eventually found a husband, the self-pity returned to change their determination into a whine. Still, he was glad to have the door between them.

This morning, as every morning, he had wakened at three. Years before, he had trained himself to get up at that time and now, in spite of his age, he never woke more than five minutes after the hour. He was proud of his early rising for he felt it showed he was not, like many of his contemporaries, relentlessly sliding into the endless blur of senility. Each morning, because he had become reconciled to the idea of dying, he felt, on the instant of his awakening, a spontaneous sense of amazement at being alive. The thought never lasted longer than the brief time between sleep and consciousness, but the good feeling lingered throughout the day.

When Fusi stepped outside, the air was cold and damp. The moon that hung low in the west was pale and fragile and very small. Fifty feet from the house, the breakwater that ran along the rear of his property loomed like the purple spine of some great beast guarding the land from a lake which seemed, in the darkness, to go on forever.

Holding his breath to still the noise of his own breathing, Fusi listened for a cough or the scuff of gravel that would mean someone was close by, watching and waiting, but the only sound was the muted rubbing of his skiff against the piling to which it was moored. Half a mile away where the land was lower, rows of gas boats roped five abreast lined the docks. The short, stubby boats with their high cabins, the grey surface of the docks and the dark water were all tinged purple from the mercury lamps. At the harbor mouth, high on a thin spire, a red light burned like a distant star.

Behind him, he heard the door open and, for a moment, he was afraid Emma might begin to shout, or worse still, turn on the back-door light and alert his enemies, but she did neither. Above all things, Emma was afraid of scandal, and would do anything to avoid causing an unsavory rumor to be attached to her own or her husband's name.

Her husband, John Smith, was as bland and inconsequential as his name. Moon-faced with wide blue eyes and a small mouth above which sat a carefully trimmed moustache, he was a head shorter than Emma and a good 50 pounds lighter. Six years before, he had been transferred to the Eddyville branch of the Bank of Montreal. His transfer from Calgary to a small town in Manitoba was the bank's way of letting him know that there would be no more promotions. He would stay in Eddyville until he retired.

A year after he arrived, Emma had married him and instead of her moving out, he had moved in. For the last two years, under Emma's prodding, John had been taking a correspondence course in theology so that when he no longer worked at the bank he could be a full-time preacher.

On the evenings when he wasn't balancing the bank's books, he labored over the multiple-choice questions in the Famous Preacher's course that he received each month from the One True and Only Word of God Church in Mobile, Alabama. Because of a freak in the atmosphere one night while she had been fiddling with the radio, Emma had heard a gospel hour advertising the course and, although neither she nor John had ever been south of Minneapolis and had never heard of the One True and Only Word of God Church before, she took it as a sign and immediately enrolled her husband in it. It cost $500.

John's notes urged him not to wait to answer His Call but to begin ministering to the needy at once for the Judgment Day was always imminent. In anticipation of the end of the world and his need for a congregation once he retired, he and Emma had become zealous missionaries, cramming their Volkswagen with a movie projector, a record-player, films, trays of slides, religious records for every occasion, posters and pamphlets, all bought or rented from the One True and Only Word of God Church. Since the townspeople were obstinately Lutheran, and since John did not want to give offence to any of his bank's customers, he and Emma hunted converts along the grey dirt roads that led past tumble-down farmhouses, the inhabitants of which were never likely to enter a bank.

Fusi did not turn to face his daughter but hurried away because he knew he had no more than an hour and a half until dawn. His legs were fine as he crossed the yard, but by the time he had mounted the steps that led over the breakwater, then climbed down fifteen feet to the shore, his left knee had begun to throb.

Holding his leg rigid to ease the pain, he waded out, loosened the ropes and heaved himself away from the shore. As soon as the boat was in deep water, he took his seat, and set both oars in the oar-locks he had carefully muffled with strips from an old shirt.

For a moment, he rested his hands on his knees, the oars rising like too-small wings from a cumbersome body, then he straightened his arms, dipped the oars cleanly into the water and in one smooth motion pulled his hands toward his chest. The first few strokes were even and graceful, but then as a speck of pain like a grain of sand formed in his shoulder, the sweep of his left oar became shorter than his right. Each time he leaned against the oars, the pain grew until it was, in his mind, a bent shingle-nail twisted and turned in his shoulder socket.

With the exertion, a ball of gas formed in his stomach, making him uncomfortable. As quickly as a balloon being blown up, it expanded until his lungs and heart were cramped and he couldn't draw in a full breath. Although the air over the lake was cool, sweat ran from his hairline.

At his two-hundredth stroke, he shipped his left oar and pulled a coil of rope with a large hook from under the seat. After checking to see that it was securely tied through the gunwale, he dropped the rope overboard and once more began to row. Normally, he would have had a buoy made from a slender tamarack pole, a block of wood and some lead weights to mark his net, but he no longer had a fishing licence so his net had to be sunk below the surface where it could not be seen by the fish inspectors.

Five more strokes of the oars and the rope went taut. He lifted both oars into the skiff, then, standing in the bow, began to pull. The boat responded sluggishly but gradually it turned and the cork line that lay hidden under two feet of water broke the surface. He grasped the net, freed the hook and began to collect the mesh until the lead line appeared. For once he had been lucky and the hook had caught the net close to one end so there was no need to backtrack.

Hand over hand he pulled, being careful not to let the corks and leads bang against the bow, for on the open water sound carried clearly for miles. In the first two fathoms there was a freshly caught pickerel. As he pulled it toward him, it beat the water with its tail, making light, slapping sounds. His fingers were cramped, but Fusi managed to catch the fish around its soft middle and, with his other hand, work the mesh free of the gills.

It was then that the pain in his knee forced him to sit. Working from the seat was awkward and cost him precious time, but he had no choice, for the pain had begun to inch up the bone toward his crotch.

He wiped his forehead with his hand and cursed his infirmity.

When he was twenty, he had thought nothing of rowing five miles from shore to lift five and six gangs of nets and then, nearly knee deep in fish, row home again. Now, he reflected bitterly, a quarter of a mile and one net were nearly beyond him. Externally, he had changed very little over the years. He was still tall and thin, his arms and legs corded with muscle. His belly was hard. His long face, with its pointed jaw, showed his age the most. That and his hands. His face was lined until it seemed there was nowhere the skin was smooth. His hands were scarred and heavily veined. His hair was grey but it was still thick.

While others were amazed at his condition, he was afraid of the changes that had taken place inside him. It was this invisible deterioration that was gradually shrinking the limits of his endurance.

Even in the darkness, he could see the distant steeple of the Lutheran church and the square bulk of the old folk's home that was directly across from his house. Emma, he thought grimly, would not be satisfied until he was safely trapped in one or carried out of the other.

He hated the old folk's home. He hated the three stories of pale yellow brick with their small, close-set windows. He hated the concrete porch with its five round pillars and the large white buckets of red geraniums. When he saw the men poking at the flowers like a bunch of old women, he pulled his blinds.

The local people who worked in the home were good to the inmates, tenants they called them, but there was no way a man could be a man in there. No whisky. Going to bed at ten. Getting up at eight. Bells for breakfast, coffee, and dinner. Bells for everything. He was surprised that they didn't have bells for going to the toilet. Someone watching over you every minute of every day. It was as if, having earned the right to be an adult, you had suddenly, in some inexplicable way, lost it again.

The porch was the worst part of the building. Long and narrow and lined with yellow and red rocking-chairs, it sat ten feet above the ground and the steps were so steep that even those who could get around all right were afraid to try them. Fusi had lived across from the old folk's home for 40 years and he had seen old people, all interchangeable as time erased their identities, shuffling and bickering their way to their deaths. Now, most of those who came out to sleep in the sun and to watch the world with glittering, jealous eyes, were people he had known.

He would have none of it. He was not afraid of dying, but he was determined that it would be in his own home. His licence had been taken from him because of his age, but he did not stop. One net was not thirty, but it was one, and a quarter-mile from shore was not five miles, but it was a quarter-mile.

He didn't shuffle and he didn't have to be fed or have a rubber diaper pinned around him each day. If anything, he had become more cunning for, time and again, the inspectors had come and destroyed the illegal nets of other fishermen, even catching and sending them to court to be fined, but they hadn't caught him for four years. Every day of the fishing season, he pitted his wits against theirs and won. At times, they had come close, but their searches had never turned up anything and, once, to his delight, when he was on the verge of being found with freshly caught fish on him, he hid them under a hole in the breakwater and then sat on the edge of the boat, talked about old times, and shared the inspectors' coffee. The memory still brought back a feeling of pleasure and excitement.

As his mind strayed over past events, he drew the boat along the net in fits and starts for his shoulder would not take the strain of steady pulling. Another good-sized fish hung limp as he pulled it to him, but then as he slipped the mesh from its head, it gave a violent shake and flew from his hands. Too stiff and slow to lunge for it, he could do nothing but watch the white flash of its belly before it struck the water and disappeared.

He paused to knead the backs of his hands, then began again. Before he was finished, his breath roared in his ears like the lake in a storm, but there were four more pickerel. With a sigh that was nearly a cry of pain, he let the net drop. Immediately, pulled down by the heavy, rusted anchors at each end, it disappeared. People were like that, he thought. One moment they were here, then they were gone and it was as if they had never been.

Behind the town, the horizon was a pale, hard grey. The silhouette of rooftops and trees might have been cut from a child's purple construction paper.

The urgent need to reach the shore before the sky became any lighter drove Fusi, for he knew that if the inspectors saw him on the water they would catch him as easily as a child. They would take his fish and net, which he did not really mind, for there were more fish in the lake and more nets in his shed, but he couldn't afford to lose his boat. His savings were not enough to buy another.

He put out the oars, only to be unable to close the fingers of his left hand. When he tried to bend his fingers around the handle, his whole arm began to tremble. Unable to do anything else, he leaned forward and pressing his fingers flat to the seat, he began to relentlessly knead them. Alternately, he prayed and cursed, trying with words to delay the sun.

"A few minutes," he whispered through clenched teeth. "Just a few minutes more." But even as he watched, the horizon turned red, then yellow and a sliver of the sun's rim rose above the houses.

Unable to wait any longer, he grabbed his left hand in his right and forced his fingers around the oar, then braced himself and began to row. Instead of cutting the water cleanly, the left oar skimmed over the surface, twisting the handle in his grip. He tried again, not letting either oar go deep. The skiff moved sluggishly ahead.

Once again, the balloon in his chest swelled and threatened to gag him, making his gorge rise, but he did not dare stop. Again and again, the left oar skipped across the surface so that the bow swung back and forth like a wounded and dying animal trying to shake away its pain. Behind him, the orange sun inched above the sharp angles of the roofs.

When the bow slid across the sand, he dropped the oars, letting them trail in the water. He grasped the gunwale, but as he climbed out, his left leg collapsed and he slid to his knees. Cold water filled his boots and soaked the legs of his trousers. Resting his head against the boat, he breathed noisily through his mouth. He remained there until gradually his breathing eased and the pain in his chest closed like a night flower touched by daylight. When he could stand, he tied the boat to one of the black pilings that was left from a breakwater that had long since been smashed and carried away.

As he collected his catch, he noticed the green fisheries department truck on the dock. He had been right. They were there. Crouching behind his boat, he waited to see if anyone was watching him. It seemed like a miracle that they had not already seen him, but he knew that they had not for if they had, their launch would have raced out of the harbor and swept down upon him.

Bending close to the sand, he limped into the deep shadow at the foot of the breakwater. They might, he knew, be waiting for him at the top of the ladder, but if they were, there was nothing he could do about it. He climbed the ladder and, hearing and seeing nothing, he rested near the top so that when he climbed into sight, he wouldn't need to sit down.

No one was in the yard. The block was empty. With a sigh of relief, he crossed to the small shed where he kept his equipment and hefted the fish onto the shelf that was nailed to one wall. He filleted his catch with care, leaving none of the translucent flesh on the backbone or skin. Then, because they were pickerel, he scooped out the cheeks, which he set aside with the roe for his breakfast.

As he carried the offal across the backyard in a bucket, the line of gulls that gathered every morning on the breakwater broke into flight and began to circle overhead. Swinging back the bucket, he flung the guts and heads and skin into the air and the gulls darted down to snatch the red entrails and iridescent heads. In a thrumming of white and grey wings, those who hadn't caught anything descended to the sand to fight for what remained.

Relieved at being rid of the evidence of his fishing—if anyone asked where he got the fillets he would say he had bought them and the other fishermen would lie for him—Fusi squatted and wiped his hands clean on the wet grass.

There was no sign of movement in the house. The blinds were still drawn and the high, narrow house with its steep roof and faded red-brick siding looked deserted. The yard was flat and bare except for the dead trunk of an elm, which was stripped bare of its bark and wind polished to the color of bone.

He returned to the shed and wrapped the fillets in a sheet of brown waxed paper, then put the roe and the cheeks into the bucket. Neither Emma nor John were up when he came in and washed the bucket and his food, but as he started cooking, Emma appeared in a quilted housecoat covered with large, purple tulips. Her head was a tangle of metal.

"Are you satisfied?" she asked, her voice trembling. "I've had no sleep since you left."

Without turning from the stove, he said, "Leave. Nobody's making you stay."

Indignantly, she answered, "And who would look after you?"

He grimaced and turned over the roe so they would be golden brown on all sides. For two weeks around Christmas, he had been sick with the flu and she never let him forget it.

"Honor thy father and mother that thy days may be long upon this earth."

He snorted out loud. What she really wanted to be sure of was that she got the house.

"You don't have to be like this," she said, starting to talk to him as if he was a child. "I only want you to stop because I care about you. All those people who live across the street, they don't. . . ."

"I'm not one of them," he barked.

"You're 70 years old. . . ."

"And I still fish," he replied angrily, cutting her off. "And I still row a boat and lift my nets. That's more than your husband can do and he's just 50." He jerked his breakfast off the stove. Because he knew it would annoy her, he began to eat out of the pan.

"I'm 70," he continued between bites, "and I beat the entire fisheries department. They catch men half my age, but they haven't caught me. Not for four years. And I fish right under their noses." He laughed with glee and laced his coffee with a finger of whisky.

Emma, her lips clamped shut and her hands clenched in fury, marched back up the stairs. In half an hour both she and John came down for their breakfast. Under Emma's glare, John cleared his throat and said, "Emma, that is we, think—" He stopped and fiddled with the knot of his tie. He always wore light grey ties and a light grey suit. "If you don't quit breaking the law, something will have to be done." He stopped and looked beseechingly at his wife, but she narrowed her eyes until little folds of flesh formed beneath them. "Perhaps something like putting you in custody so you'll be saved from yourself."

Fusi was so shocked that for once he could think of nothing to say. Encouraged by his silence, John said, "It will be for your own good."

Before either of them realized what he was up to, Fusi leaned sideways and emptied his cup into his son-in-law's lap.

The coffee was hot. John flung himself backward with a screech, but the back legs of his chair caught on a crack in the linoleum and he tipped over with a crash. In the confusion Fusi stalked upstairs.

In a moment he flung an armload of clothes down. When his daughter rushed to the bottom of the stairs, Fusi flung another armload of clothes at her.

"This is my house," he bellowed. "You're not running it yet."

Emma began grabbing clothes and laying them flat so they wouldn't wrinkle. John, both hands clenched between his legs, hobbled over to stare.

Fusi descended the stairs and they parted to let him by. At the counter, he picked up the package of fish and turning toward them, said, "I want you out of here when I get back or I'll go out on the lake and get caught and tell everyone that you put me up to it."

His fury was so great that once he was outside he had to lean against the house while a spasm of trembling swept over him. When he was composed, he rounded the corner. At one side of the old folk's home there was an enclosed fire escape that curled to the ground like a piece of intestine. He headed for the kitchen door under it.

Fusi had kept on his rubber boots, dark slacks and red turtleneck sweater, and because he knew that behind the curtains, eyes were watching his every move, he tried to hide the stiffness in his left leg.

Although it was early, Rosie Melysyn was already at work. She always came first, never missing a day. She was a large, good natured widow with grey hair.

"How are you today, Mr. Bergman?" she asked.

"Fine," he replied. "I'm feeling great." He held out the brown paper package. "I thought some of the old people might like some fish." Although he had brought fish for the last four years, he always said the same thing.

Rosie dusted off her hands, took the package and placed it on the counter.

"I'll see someone gets it," she assured him. "Help yourself to some coffee."

As he took the pot from the stove, she asked, "No trouble with the inspectors?"

He always waited for her to ask that. He grinned delightedly, the pain of the morning already becoming a memory. "No trouble. They'll never catch me. I'm up too early. I saw them hanging about, but it didn't do them any good."

"Jimmy Henderson died last night," Rosie offered.

"Jimmy Henderson," Fusi repeated. They had been friends, but he felt no particular sense of loss. Jimmy had been in the home for three years. "I'm not surprised. He wasn't more than 68 but he had given up. You give up, you're going to die. You believe in yourself and you can keep right on going."

Rosie started mixing oatmeal and water.

"You know," he said to her broad back, "I was with Jimmy the first time he got paid. He cut four cords of wood for 60¢ and spent it all on hootch. He kept running up and down the street and flapping his arms, trying to fly. When he passed out, we hid him in the hayloft of the stable so his old man couldn't find him."

Rosie tried to imagine Jimmy Henderson attempting to fly and failed. To her, he was a bent man with a sad face who had to use a walker to get to the dining room. What she remembered about him best was coming on him unexpectedly and finding him silently crying. He had not seen her and she had quietly backed away.

Fusi was lingering because after he left, there was a long day ahead of him. He would have the house to himself and after checking the vacated room to see that nothing of his had been taken, he would tie his boat properly, sleep for three hours, then eat lunch. In the afternoon he would make a trip to the docks to see what the inspectors were up to and collect information about their movements.

The back door opened with a swish and he felt a cool draft. Both he and Rosie turned to look. He was shocked to see that instead of it being one of the kitchen help, it was Emma. She shut the door and glanced at them both, then at the package of fish.

"What do you want?" he demanded.

"I called the inspectors," she replied, "to tell them you're not responsible for yourself. I told them about the net."

He gave a start, but then was relieved when he remembered they had to actually catch him fishing before they could take the skiff. "So what?" he asked, confident once more.

Quietly, she replied, "You don't have to worry about being caught. They've known about your fishing all along."

Suddenly frightened by her calm certainty, his voice rose as he said, "That's not true."

"They don't care," she repeated. "Inspector McKenzie was the name of the one I talked to. He said you couldn't do any harm with one net. They've been watching you every morning just in case you should get into trouble and need help."

Emma stood there, not moving, her head tipped back, her eyes benevolent.

He turned to Rosie. "She's lying, isn't she? That's not true. They wouldn't do that?"

"Of course, she's lying," Rosie assured him.

He would have rushed outside but Emma was standing in his way. Since he could not get past her, he fled through the swinging doors that led to the dining room.

As the doors shut, Rosie turned on Emma and said, "You shouldn't have done that." She picked up the package of fish with its carefully folded wrapping. In the artificial light, the package glowed like a piece of amber. She held it cupped in the hollows of her hands. "You had no right."

Emma seemed to grow larger and her eyes shone.

"The Lord's work be done," she said, her right hand partly raised as if she were preparing to give a benediction.

RESPONSE

1. Select four statements from the story which explain why Fusi continues to fish in spite of his daughter's objections.

2. Do you know anyone like Fusi? Give an oral characterization of that person.

3. Using specific sentences from the story, determine what motivates Emma's behaviour towards her father. Do you agree with these sentiments? Why or why not?

4. Do you agree with Rosie when she says to Emma, "You shouldn't have done that . . . You had no right"? Explain.

EXTENSION

5. Interview the oldest person you know. Gently try to determine that person's hopes and fears. Share your findings in a small group and explain what you have learned. Record the experience in a journal entry.

Our Aging Society

Charles A. White

In what ways do people over age 65 have an impact on people under age 20?

Do you think our society treats senior citizens appropriately? Explain.

The Greying of Canada

At the end of World War II, Canada's population was about 12 million. By 1961, it had reached 18 million. Most of the growth in those 15 years came from the biggest baby boom Canada has ever seen. There were similar booms elsewhere, but, according to actuary Robert Brown, ours was the biggest anywhere—a "tidal wave."

Since then, the birth rate has dived from its high of 3.8 children per family to the current 1.67. Meanwhile, that six-million-strong generation of baby boomers has formed a moving bulge in the population. By 2010, the first of the baby boomers will be coming up for retirement. By 2025, the last of them will enter the senior ranks.

It all adds up to an aging Canadian society. Not enough babies are being born to maintain the balance. A very large, concentrated group is steadily aging. And, last but not least, people are living longer.

Already Canada, though a young nation, has a higher proportion of elderly than any other industrial country. About 10% of us (well over two million people) is over 65, up from 8.1% in 1971. Those numbers will rise steadily. Statistics Canada reports that more than four million Canadians will be elderly by the turn of the century. By 2031, there will be seven million seniors, "an astonishing 27% of the population."

Certain factors could upset the prediction, of course. A rise in the birth rate would tilt the balance back towards youth. So would an immigration policy which brought in large numbers of younger people.

If we assume that birth rate and immigration changes will be minor, however, we know now that our population will age relentlessly. These facts are changing society now and will change it far more in the future. Here's why:

- Many elderly people are prosperous and self-supporting. However, many others depend on public pensions and need care, either in institutions or through community services. Canadians in the work-force must pay for this through their taxes.
- At present, there are five workers for every pensioner, so the burden is not too great. By 2031, the ratio will have changed to only two workers for each pensioner.

Government planners must prepare now to meet this huge challenge of our aging society.

Granny-bashers Beware

The growing numbers of seniors give them potential to make or unmake governments on election day. Until recently they had been unorganized, but that is changing. During the last 10 years, the "Grey Panthers" have become a powerful lobby for senior concerns in the United States. Politicians in Washington are listening and adjusting.

In Canada, Ottawa got its first taste of how explosive grey power can be two years ago. The fuse was lit by Finance Minister Michael Wilson. He wanted to make a partial cut in the Old Age Pension (OAP). Mr. Wilson quickly found he had stirred up a hornet's nest.

Canada's seniors mobilized to defeat the "granny-bashers." Leaders of groups from across the country marched on Ottawa. There was the National Pensioners and Senior Citizens Organization, with 400,000 members. There was Canadian Pensioners Concerned. There was the Canadian Council of Retirees. Together they raised a howl that echoed around the halls of Parliament.

Suddenly, pensioners were in demand for telephone interviews, radio talk shows, and in community halls. Mr. Wilson's attack on pensions, they said, would put another 100,000 to 200,000 seniors below the poverty line.

Ed Broadbent, New Democratic Party leader, was quick to join the crusade. In the end, however, the seniors would have done it on their own. Stunned by the united protest from British Columbia to Newfoundland, the Conservatives crumbled on the pension issue. The OAP would remain unchanged.

With its landmark victory, grey power had entered the equation; politics in Canada would never be quite the same again.

What the Boomers Want the Boomers Get

Spending patterns are changing, along with everything else, as Canadian society ages. With increasing numbers, older citizens as consumers are going to have more and more to say about what happens in the marketplace.

Watching the baby boomers' progress through the decades, gives a fascinating study in shifting consumer markets.

In the '50s, baby-care manuals by Dr. Benjamin Spock and diaper services were big items. In the '60s, as the "boomies" moved into their teens, million-selling pop records and jeans flooded the market. By the '70s, the maturing boomers still wanted their jeans. So, makers such as Levi, re-designed their products with a little more room in the seat and thigh. In the '80s, the well-educated boomer generation is a prime market for books, movies, VCRs, cars, and housing.

The first baby boomers have turned 40, and more change is on the way. They won't give up youth easily, predicts Dr. Ken Dychtwald, author of several books on aging. Cosmetic surgery will be a growth industry, and instead of the greying of North America "it may be the tinting of North America."

Marketers must be fast on their feet to make the most of the rapid shifts in consumer demand. Johnson & Johnson has been pitching commercials to adults for its baby powder since the mid-'60s. Mattel has moved into adult video games for new revenue. McDonald's breakfasts for working adults are aimed at the over-55s. And soft drink manufacturers are testing the appeal of mineral water for health-conscious seniors.

The senior market is alive, well, and growing fast. Many retirees are finding they have more money than ever before.

The children are gone, the mortgage is paid off. Pensions, retirement saving plans, and dividends are rolling in. They have money to spend and are ready to spend it on travel, cars, and other items of gracious living.

People with things to sell don't want to be caught napping. Real estate developers are offering seniors the good life in special retirement communities. Builders are providing separate "granny apartments" in or near the homes of younger families.

Merchandisers, such as shoe repair shops and dry cleaners are tempting pensioners with discounts. Financial advisers are putting together special investment packages for older clients. Brokers are recommending the stocks of companies, such as nursing home operators, which cater to seniors' needs.

What we're seeing here is only the beginning. While most marketing is still youth oriented, future domination of supply and demand will belong to Canada's elderly.

The Poor Elderly

Retirement may be the best of times for seniors with money to smooth the bumps. For half of Canada's 2.7 million elderly, it is the worst of times. These are the seniors with incomes so low they also receive federal and/or provincial income supplements on top of Old Age Security.

For the people who have slipped through the holes in the social security net life is difficult. They are the 45% of the population who don't have private pension plans. They are the thousands who held part-time jobs with no fringe benefits. They are the many others whose earnings have been too low to allow them to save for retirement. They are the self-employed.

Above all, these seniors who live close to or below the poverty line are women. In spite of the drive for pay equality, women are still at the low end of the wage scale. More than two thirds of them have never worked for pay or have worked only part-time.

Because women live longer than men, widows loom large among the elderly poor. In many cases, the husband's private pension, if he had one, has died along with him. He may have saved little and had no life insurance.

The widow is left with a house to maintain or the rent to pay and not much to do it with. To stretch her income, she must often spend hours in search of bargains, get her clothes at a Salvation Army store, and line up at a food bank for handouts or go hungry.

Bare survival is the lot of the bottom half of the elderly in Canada. For these men and women, poverty and neglect make the latter end of life a grim struggle.

—Canada and the World, October 1987

RESPONSE

1. Summarize the continuing effects of the Baby Boom generation on Canadian society.

2. In what ways must the Canadian government prepare to meet the "huge challenge" of an aging society?

3. a) Should there be a mandatory retirement age? Explain.
   b) If so, what do you think is the optimum age for mandatory retirement? Explain.

EXTENSION

4. Research the statistics on the age of the Canadian population. Explain to the class what these statistics imply about our population in the year 2010. How will this affect society?

The Thrill of the Grass

W. P. Kinsella

> What elicits feelings of nostalgia from you? Explain.

1981: the summer the baseball players went on strike. The dull weeks drag by, the summer deepens, the strike is nearly a month old. Outside the city the corn rustles and ripens in the sun. Summer without baseball: a disruption to the psyche. An unexplainable aimlessness engulfs me. I stay later and later each evening in the small office at the rear of my shop. Now, driving home after work, the worst of the rush hour traffic over, it is the time of evening I would normally be heading for the stadium.

I enjoy arriving an hour early, parking in a far corner of the lot, walking slowly toward the stadium, rays of sun dropping softly over my shoulders like tangerine ropes, my shadow gliding with me, black as an umbrella. I like to watch young families beside their campers, the mothers in shorts, grilling hamburgers, their men drinking beer. I enjoy seeing little boys dressed in the home team uniform, barely toddling, clutching hotdogs in upraised hands.

I am a failed shortstop. As a young man, I saw myself diving to my left, graceful as a toppling tree, fielding high grounders like a cat leaping for butterflies, bracing my right foot and tossing to first, the throw true as if a steel ribbon connected my hand and the first baseman's glove. I dreamed of leading the American League in hitting—being inducted into the Hall of Fame. I batted .217 in my senior year of high school and averaged 1.3 errors per nine innings.

I know the stadium will be deserted; nevertheless I wheel my car down off the freeway, park, and walk across the silent lot, my footsteps rasping and mournful. Strangle-grass and creeping charlie are already inching up through the gravel, surreptitious, surprised at their own ease. Faded bottle caps, rusted bits of chrome, an occasional paper clip, recede into the earth. I circle a ticket booth, sun-faded, empty, the door closed by an oversized padlock. I walk beside the tall, machinery-green, board fence. A half mile away a few cars hiss along the freeway; overhead a single-engine plane fizzes lazily. The whole place is silent as an empty classroom, like a house suddenly without children.

It is then that I spot the door-shape. I have to check twice to be sure it is there: a door cut in the deep green boards of the fence, more the promise of a door than the real thing, the kind of door, as children, we cut in the sides of cardboard boxes with our mother's paring knives. As I move closer, a golden circle of lock, like an acrimonious eye, establishes its certainty.

I stand, my nose so close to the door I can smell the faint odour of paint, the golden eye of a lock inches from my own eyes. My desire to be inside the ballpark is so great that for the first time in my life I commit a criminal act. I have been a locksmith for over forty years. I take the small tools from the pocket of my jacket, and in less time than it would take a speedy runner to circle the bases I am inside the stadium. Though the ballpark is open-air, it smells of abandonment; the walkways and seating areas are cold as basements. I breathe the odours of rancid popcorn and wilted cardboard.

The maintenance staff were laid off when the strike began. Synthetic grass does not need to be cut or watered. I stare down at the ball diamond, where just to the right of the pitcher's mound, a single weed, perhaps two inches high, stands defiant in the rain-pocked dirt.

The field sits breathless in the orangy glow of the evening sun. I stare at the potato-coloured earth of the infield, that wide, dun arc, surrounded by plastic grass. As I contemplate the prickly turf, which scorches the thighs and buttocks of a sliding player as if he were being seared by hot steel, it stares back in its uniform ugliness. The seams that send routinely hit ground balls veering at tortuous angles, are vivid, grey as scars.

I remember the ballfields of my childhood, the outfields full of soft hummocks and brown-eyed gopher holes.

I stride down from the stands and walk out to the middle of the field. I touch the stubble that is called grass, take off my shoes, but find it is like walking on a row of toothbrushes. It was an evil day when they stripped the sod from this ballpark, cut it into yard-wide swathes, rolled it, memories and all, into great green-and-black cinnamonroll shapes, trucked it away. Nature temporarily defeated. But Nature is patient.

Over the next few days an idea forms within me, ripening, swelling, pushing everything else into a corner. It is like knowing a new, wonderful joke and not being able to share. I need an accomplice.

I go to see a man I don't know personally, though I have seen his face peering at me from the financial pages of the local newspaper, and the *Wall Street Journal*, and I have been watching his profile at the baseball stadium, two boxes to the right of me, for several years. He is a fan. Really a fan. When the weather is intemperate, or the game not close, the people around us disappear like flowers closing at sunset, but we are always there until the last pitch. I know he is a man who attends because of the beauty and mystery of the game, a man who can sit during the last of the ninth with the game decided innings ago, and draw joy from watching the first baseman adjust the angle of his glove as the pitcher goes into his windup.

He, like me, is a first-base-side fan. I've always watched baseball from behind first base. The positions fans choose at sporting events are like politics, religion, or philosophy: a view of the world, a way of seeing the universe. They make no sense to anyone, have no basis in anything but stubbornness.

I brought up my daughters to watch baseball from the first-base side. One lives in Japan and sends me box scores from Japanese newspapers, and Japanese baseball magazines with pictures of superstars politely bowing to one another. She has a season ticket in Yokohama; on the first-base side.

"Tell him a baseball fan is here to see him," is all I will say to his secretary. His office is in a skyscraper, from which he can look out over the city to where the prairie rolls green as mountain water to the limits of the eye. I wait all afternoon in the artificially cool, glassy reception area with its yellow and mauve chairs, chrome and glass coffee tables. Finally, in the late afternoon, my message is passed along.

"I've seen you at the baseball stadium," I say, not introducing myself.

"Yes," he says. "I recognize you. Three rows back, about eight seats to my left. You have a red scorebook and you often bring your daughter . . ."

"Granddaughter. Yes, she goes to sleep in my lap in the late innings, but she knows how to calculate an ERA and she's only in Grade 2."

"One of my greatest regrets," says this tall man, whose moustache and carefully styled hair are polar-bear white, "is that my grandchildren all live over a thousand miles away. You're very lucky. Now, what can I do for you?"

"I have an idea," I say. "One that's been creeping toward me like a first baseman when the bunt sign is on. What do you think about artificial turf?"

"Hmmmf," he snorts, "that's what the strike should be about. Baseball is meant to be played on summer evenings and Sunday afternoons, on grass just cut by a horse-drawn mower," and we smile as our eyes meet.

"I've discovered the ballpark is open, to me anyway," I go on. "There's no one there while the strike is on. The wind blows through the high top of the grandstand, whining until the pigeons in the rafters flutter. It's lonely as a ghost town."

"And what is it you do there, alone with the pigeons?"

"I dream."

"And where do I come in?"

"You've always struck me as a man who dreams. I think we have things in common. I think you might like to come with me. I could show you what I dream, paint you pictures, suggest what might happen . . ."

He studies me carefully for a moment, like a pitcher trying to decide if he can trust the sign his catcher has just given him.

"Tonight?" he says. "Would tonight be too soon?"

"Park in the northwest corner of the lot about 1:00 a.m.. There is a door about fifty yards to the right of the main gate. I'll open it when I hear you."

He nods.

I turn and leave.

The night is clear and cotton warm when he arrives. "Oh, my," he says, staring at the stadium turned chrome-blue by a full moon. "Oh, my," he says again, breathing in the faint odours of baseball, the reminder of fans and players not long gone.

"Let's go down to the field," I say. I am carrying a cardboard pizza box, holding it on the upturned palms of my hands, like an offering.

When we reach the field, he first stands on the mound, makes an awkward attempt at a windup, then does a little sprint from first to about half-way to second. "I think I know what you've brought," he says, gesturing toward the box, "but let me see anyway."

I open the box in which rests a square foot of sod, the grass smooth and pure, cool as a swatch of satin, fragile as baby's hair.

"Ohhh," the man says, reaching out a finger to test the moistness of it. "Oh, I see."

We walk across the field, the harsh, prickly turf making the bottoms of my feet tingle, to the left-field corner where, in the angle formed by the foul line and the warning track, I lay down the square foot of sod. "That's beautiful," my friend says, kneeling beside me, placing his hand, fingers spread wide, on the verdant square, leaving a print faint as a veronica.

I take from my belt a sickle-shaped blade, the kind used for cutting carpet. I measure along the edge of the sod, dig the point in and pull carefully toward me. There is a ripping sound, like tearing an old bed sheet. I hold up the square of artificial turf like something freshly killed, while all the time digging the sharp point into the packed earth I have exposed. I replace the sod lovingly, covering the newly bared surface.

"A protest," I say.

"But it could be more," the man replies.

"I hoped you'd say that. It could be. If you'd like to come back . . ."

"Tomorrow night?"

"Tomorrow night would be fine. But there will be an admission charge . . ."

"A square of sod?"

"A square of sod two inches thick . . ."

"Of the same grass?"

"Of the same grass. But there's more."

"I suspected as much."

"You must have a friend . . ."

"Who would join us?"

"Yes."

"I have two. Would that be all right?"

"I trust your judgement."

"My father. He's over eighty," my friend says. "You might have seen him with me once or twice. He lives over fifty miles from here, but if I call him he'll come. And my friend . . ."

"If they pay their admission they'll be welcome . . ."

"And *they* may have friends . . ."

"Indeed they may. But what will we do with this?" I say, holding up the sticky-backed square of turf, which smells of glue and fabric.

"We could mail them anonymously to baseball executives, politicians, clergymen."

"Gentle reminders not to tamper with Nature."

We dance toward the exit, rampant with excitement.

"You will come back? You'll bring others?"

"Count on it," says my friend.

They do come, those trusted friends, and friends of friends, each making a live, green deposit. At first, a tiny row of sod squares begins to inch along toward left-centre field. The next night even more people arrive, the following night more again, and the night after there is positively a crowd. Those who come once seem always to return accompanied by friends, occasionally a son or young brother, but mostly men my age or older, for we are the ones who remember the grass.

Night after night the pilgrimage continues. The first night I stand inside the deep green door, listening. I hear a vehicle stop; hear a car door close with a snug thud. I open the door when the sound of soft soled shoes on gravel tells me it is time. The door swings silent as a snake. We nod curt greetings to each other. Two men pass me, each carrying a grasshopper-legged sprinkler. Later, each sprinkler will sizzle like frying onions as it wheels, a silver sparkler in the moonlight.

During the nights that follow, I stand sentinel-like at the top of the grandstand, watching as my cohorts arrive. Old men walking across a parking lot in a row, in the dark, carrying coiled hoses, looking like the many wheels of a locomotive, old men who have slipped away from their homes, skulked down their sturdy sidewalks, breathing the cool, grassy, after-midnight air. They have left behind their sleeping, grey-haired women, their immaculate bungalows, their manicured lawns. They continue to walk across the parking lot, while occasionally a soft wheeze, a nibbling, breathy sound like an old horse might make, divulges their humanity. They move methodically toward the baseball stadium which hulks against the moon-blue sky like a small mountain. Beneath the tint of starlight, the tall light standards which rise above the fences and grandstand glow purple, necks bent forward, like sunflowers heavy with seed.

My other daughter lives in this city, is married to a fan, but one who watches baseball from behind third base. And like marrying outside the faith, she has been converted to the third-base side. They have their own season tickets, twelve rows up just to the outfield side of third base. I love her, but I don't trust her enough to let her in on my secret.

I could trust my granddaughter, but she is too young. At her age she shouldn't have to face such responsibility. I remember my own daughter, the one who lives in Japan, remember her at nine, all knees, elbows and missing teeth—remember peering in her room, seeing her asleep, a shower of well-thumbed baseball cards scattered over her chest and pillow.

I haven't been able to tell my wife—it is like my compatriots and I are involved in a ritual for true believers only. Maggie, who knew me when I still dreamed of playing professionally myself— Maggie, after over half a lifetime together, comes and sits in my lap in the comfortable easy chair which has adjusted through the years to my thickening shape, just as she has. I love to hold the lightness of her, her tongue exploring my mouth, gently as a baby's finger.

"Where do you go?" she asks sleepily when I crawl into bed at dawn.

I mumble a reply. I know she doesn't sleep well when I'm gone. I can feel her body rhythms change as I slip out of bed after midnight.

"Aren't you too old to be having a change of life," she says, placing her toast-warm hand on my cold thigh.

I am not the only one with this problem.

"I'm developing a reputation," whispers an affable man at the ballpark. "I imagine any number of private investigators following any number of cars across the city. I imagine them creeping about the parking lot, shining pen-lights on licence plates, trying to guess what we're up to. Think of the reports they must prepare. I wonder if our wives are disappointed that we're not out discoing with frizzy-haired teenagers?"

Night after night, virtually no words are spoken. Each man seems to know his assignment. Not all bring sod. Some carry rakes, some hoes, some hoses, which, when joined together, snake across the infield and outfield, dispensing the blessing of water. Others, cradle in their arms bags of earth for building up the infield to meet the thick, living sod.

I often remain high in the stadium, looking down on the men moving over the earth, dark as ants, each sodding, cutting, watering, shaping. Occasionally the moon finds a knife blade as it trims the sod or slices away a chunk of artificial turf, and tosses the reflection skyward like a bright ball. My body tingles. There should be symphony music playing. Everyone should be humming "America The Beautiful."

Toward dawn, I watch the men walking away in groups, like small patrols of soldiers, carrying instead of arms, the tools and utensils which breathe life back into the arid ballfield.

Row by row, night by night, we lay the little squares of sod, moist as chocolate cake with green icing. Where did all the sod come from? I picture many men, in many parts of the city, surreptitiously cutting chunks out of their own lawns in the leafy midnight darkness, listening to the uncomprehending protests of their wives the next day—pretending to know nothing of it—pretending to have called the police to investigate.

When the strike is over I know we will all be here to watch the workouts, to hear the recalcitrant joints crackling like twigs after the forced inactivity. We will sit in our regular seats, scattered like popcorn throughout the stadium, and we'll nod as we pass on the way to the exits, exchange secret smiles, proud as new fathers.

For me, the best part of all will be the surprise. I feel like a magician who has gestured hypnotically and produced an elephant from thin air. I know I am not alone in my wonder. I know that rockets shoot off in half-a-hundred chests, the excitement of birthday mornings, Christmas eves, and home-town doubleheaders, boils within each of my conspirators. Our secret rites have been performed with love, like delivering a valentine to a sweetheart's door in that blue-steel span of morning just before dawn.

Players and management are meeting round the clock. A settlement is imminent. I have watched the stadium covered square foot by square foot until it looks like green graph paper. I have stood and felt the cool odours of the grass rise up and touch my face. I have studied the lines between each small square, watched those lines fade until they were visible to my eyes alone, then not even to them.

What will the players think, as they straggle into the stadium and find the miracle we have created? The old-timers will raise their heads like ponies, as far away as the parking lot, when the thrill of the grass reaches their nostrils. And, as they dress, they'll recall sprawling in the lush outfields of childhood, the grass as cool as a mother's hand on a forehead.

"Goodbye, goodbye," we say at the gate, the smell of water, of sod, of sweat, small perfumes in the air. Our secrets are safe with each other. We go our separate ways.

Alone in the stadium in the last chill darkness before dawn, I drop to my hands and knees in the centre of the outfield. My palms are sodden. Water touches the skin between my spread fingers. I lower my face to the silvered grass, which, wonder of wonders, already has the ephemeral odours of baseball about it.

RESPONSE

1. What is the narrator implying when he refers to his actions as "a protest"? Explain.

2. Why does the narrator conceal his activities from Maggie?

3. a) Why are the characters in the story so enthralled by baseball?
   b) Has the author overstated their devotion to the game? Explain.

4. In what ways has the game of baseball been demeaned by business and technology?

EXTENSION

5. Explain how another sport has been improved or degraded by business and technology.

6. Write a personal essay demonstrating how your life has benefited from your involvement in sports.

Our Biological Clock

Carolyn Parrish

> What methods and activities do some people use to delay the aging process? Do you think any of these methods and activities are effective? Explain.

In the 18th century it was believed that people aged because they lost vital particles every time they exhaled.

Despite hundreds of years of research into aging, we're still not much closer to halting the process. Live fast, die young and only then can you avoid the slow decay.

Aging affects individuals at different rates. However, on average, most human beings are hit with roughly the same symptoms at roughly the same time.

Warnings begin to appear in the 30s. At this point, the body begins to lose about 1% of its efficiency every year.

The over-the-hill jokes start at about 40. Lines and wrinkles are forming along the grooves of common facial expressions. Crabby people look crabby—even when they sleep. Crows' feet have settled in the corners of eyes, the result of years of squinting against the sun. Arcs linking the nostrils to the sides of the mouth punish those who have smiled a lot.

Body length begins to decrease between the ages of 30 and 40, with an average shrinkage of 6 mm. People have withstood gravity to this point, but muscles now begin to weaken and the disks between the bones of the spine deteriorate. The average person will lose between 38 mm and 50 mm in height by the age of 70.

Men gradually produce fewer hormones over their entire adult lives. However, women get a sudden sign of approaching old age in the mid- to late-40s—menopause. One in five women suffer from depression and severe physical symptoms, as the ovaries produce less estrogen.

Women also begin losing minerals and calcium from their bones. This causes bones to soften or become brittle and break easily—a condition known as *osteoporosis*.

In the mid- to late-40s, men and women whose eyesight has always been good, suddenly have difficulty reading. In an attempt to focus, printed pages are held farther and farther away. Known as *presbyopia*, this condition is a result of the lens losing flexibility and becoming more rigid. Reading glasses become a necessity.

Men have unique problems. They actually get hairier with age but, alas, not where it does them much good. Hair grows in the ears, in the nostrils, and on the back. Eyebrows become thicker. On top of the head though, something else is going on.

Balding begins at the temples, and then at the "monk's circle" at the back of the head. The two spots eventually meet, leaving the top of the head bare and vulnerable to the sun, bird droppings and the nasty jibes of those fortunate enough to have kept their hair. The gene that causes balding is carried by females and passed on to their offspring.

The fact is that the 40s is the first fork in the road to old age. Accelerating through the 50s and 60s, the ravages of time become more obvious.

The skin becomes thinner and spreads out, much like a baggy suit. Folds settle under the eyes and chin as the cheeks begin to sag. Dark "liver spots" of pigment often appear on the hands and face.

Stamina and strength ebb with the years. The weakening of the heart, lungs and muscles means less oxygen enters the body. The heart is slower dispersing this oxygen through the bloodstream to the muscles. Although the heart rate doesn't change, the beats get weaker as the heart muscles age.

A healthy 70-year-old can run a marathon, but it will take at least one hour longer than it did at 30. The race will have to be held in daylight though. This is because peripheral (side) vision is greatly reduced and night vision is almost gone.

Hardening of the arteries goes on throughout life. Fat builds up in the lining of the arteries. With calcium, the fat forms a sludge which restricts the flow of blood. Women who are no longer protected by their natural hormones, also succumb to heart attacks.

Heart disease and strokes will kill almost half the over-60s. Those who survive will have further changes in appearance.

With age, facial features actually get bigger. Cartilage begins to accumulate so that, by 70, noses are 13 mm wider and 13 mm longer. Earlobes fatten and droop 6 mm longer.

The skull thickens so the circumference of the head is greater. At the same time, the brain shrinks, losing millions of neurons over the years. This cell loss varies in different parts of the brain. The region that controls sleep is very hard hit. So, the elderly sleep about two hours less per night than they did in their 40s.

At 50, a slight loss of memory begins. Dr. Christopher Patterson, head of geriatric medicine at McMaster University in Hamilton, calls this "benign forgetfulness." Memory doesn't drop off rapidly in healthy people, it dwindles gradually.

Dr. Marion Diamond, of the University of California at Berkeley, has discovered that memory loss is preventable. In studies with rats she has found that old nerve endings can actually grow branches when the subjects are exposed to new and stimulating experiences.

A growing number of people suffering from senile dementia (almost total loss of memory, and confusion) are suffering from Alzheimer's disease. Rapid loss of brain function occurs as the disease progresses. There is a loss of thinking, reasoning, speech and body control.

Alzheimer's eventually leads to death. It's the fifth most frequent killer after heart disease, cancer, strokes, and accidents. After many years of study, the cause, treatment, and cure are still unknown.

In a society devoted to the worship of all that is young, 70 is not an age to look forward to: wrinkles, flab, liver spots, large noses, receding gums, long, yellow teeth, and hairy nostrils. Aging is only endured because the alternative is worse. What have scientists done about the fate we all share?

The average lifespan of North Americans has risen from 47 in 1900 to 73 for someone born today. This gain reflects progress in eliminating premature death, rather than increasing the life of the average person. Fewer people die young, yet only a tiny number reach 100. The greatest authenticated age in the world was 117, recorded in Japan.

Specialists maintain that our hearts and lungs were not

designed for a very long life. Research shows that the first deposits of fat in the heart's aorta are found in the pre-teen years.

Scientists have found that each species seems to have a characteristic lifespan. A housefly is ancient at six weeks, a mouse at three years, a robin at 10, and an elephant at 70.

In nature, species live long enough to reproduce and usually die soon after breeding. But, humans have learned how to manipulate their environment and live longer than is necessary to breed and rear children. People now live long enough to experience the wear and tear of time.

Most people who study aging believe the normal lifespan of humans will always be less than 100 years. They have reached this conclusion by looking into how cells, the building blocks of the body, divide and reproduce.

When cells from the lung of a human fetus are cultured in a laboratory they will divide and multiply, within limits. After a period of vigorous growth, they slow, show signs of change and then die out. Cells from an older donor grow for a shorter period. The fetal cells double roughly 50 times; the adult cells, 20.

Experiments such as this give clues to what happens in living bodies. If aging is planned, what governs the process? Scientists agree the answer must lie at the very heart of cells. The genetic blueprint (DNA) carries the instructions for how life begins, for the development of the fetus in the womb, for the growth into adulthood, and for the decline of old age.

Some scientists believe in a "passive" theory. They think that nature created aging by error rather than design. DNA is exposed to environmental damage, particularly the ultraviolet radiation from the sun. The immune system, made up of tiny cells called "T" cells, is our protection against disease.

Although old people have as many "T" cells as young ones, those of the elderly are often defective. This leaves them more likely to succumb to diseases such as pneumonia.

Other scientists believe in an "active" theory. This says that a specific gene carries the program for aging and death. This gene kicks in as early as the onset of sexual maturity. It ensures death by gradually shutting down the body's systems, thereby keeping the human population in balance. Although many biologists have spent years searching for this elusive gene, no one has yet found it.

Can youth spring eternal? Can aging be slowed? Again, there are two schools of thought. Those who believe each cell is shut down at a predetermined time, suggest it's impossible to lengthen the lifespan by much. The other school of thought feels that humans have the power to slow down the process that wears cells out; they just haven't conquered it yet.

Several truths are known, however. Some people age better than others—those who have long-lived parents, a satisfying job and plenty of money. Those who are married live longer than those who are not. Those who exercise moderately, drink alcohol moderately, and eat moderately last longer. Those who avoid smoking, stress and the sun tend to reach bigger ages.

The answer seems to be: Relax, hope you have the right genes, and accept peacefully the aging of your body.

RESPONSE

1. Based on the author's description, what aspects of the aging process surprised you the most? Explain.

2. How could the way you live your life now damage the condition of your health thirty years from now?

3. According to the essay, what should you do to live a long and healthy life?

EXTENSION

4. With a partner or in a small group, discuss how an irresponsible attitude towards your personal health could affect society.

5. Write a journal entry about the more pleasant aspects of aging that you are looking forward to.

Come Lady Death

Peter S. Beagle

> List and discuss the ways in which death has been traditionally personified.
>
> What is boredom? List and discuss the ways in which people attempt to avoid boredom.

This all happened in England a long time ago, when that George who spoke English with a heavy German accent and hated his sons was King. At that time there lived in London a lady who had nothing to do but give parties. Her name was Floa, Lady Neville, and she was a widow and very old. She lived in a great house not far from Buckingham Palace, and she had so many servants that she could not possibly remember all their names; indeed, there were some she had never even seen. She had more food than she could eat, more gowns than she could ever wear; she had wine in her cellars that no one would drink in her lifetime, and her private vaults were filled with great works of art that she did not know she owned. She spent the last years of her life giving parties and balls to which the greatest lords of England—and sometimes the King himself—came, and she was known as the wisest and wittiest woman in all London.

But in time her own parties began to bore her and though she invited the most famous people in the land and hired the greatest jugglers and acrobats and dancers and magicians to entertain them, still she found her parties duller and duller. Listening to court gossip, which she had always loved, made her yawn. The most marvelous music, the most exciting feat of magic put her to sleep. Watching a beautiful young couple dance by her made her feel sad, and she hated to feel sad.

And so, one summer afternoon she called her closest friends

around her and said to them, "More and more I find that my parties entertain everyone but me. The secret of my long life is that nothing has ever been dull for me. For all my life, I have been interested in everything I saw and been anxious to see more. But I cannot stand to be bored, and I will not go to parties at which I expect to be bored, especially if they are my own. Therefore, to my next ball I shall invite the one guest I am sure no one, not even myself, could possibly find boring. My friends, the guest of honor at my next party shall be Death himself!"

A young poet thought that this was a wonderful idea, but the rest of her friends were terrified and drew back from her. They did not want to die, they pleaded with her. Death would come for them when he was ready; why should she invite him before the appointed hour, which would arrive soon enough? But Lady Neville said, "Precisely. If Death has planned to take any of us on the night of my party, he will come whether he is invited or not. But if none of us are to die, then I think it would be charming to have Death among us—perhaps even to perform some little trick if he is in a good humor. And think of being able to say that we had been to a party with Death! All of London will envy us, all of England."

The idea began to please her friends, but a young lord, very new to London, suggested timidly, "Death is so busy. Suppose he has work to do and cannot accept your invitation?"

"No one has ever refused an invitation of mine," said Lady Neville, "not even the King." And the young lord was not invited to her party.

She sat down then and there and wrote out the invitation. There was some dispute among her friends as to how they should address Death. "His Lordship Death" seemed to place him only on the level of a viscount or a baron. "His Grace Death" met with more acceptance, but Lady Neville said it sounded hypocritical. And to refer to Death as "His Majesty" was to make him the equal of the King of England, which even Lady Neville would not dare to do. It was finally decided that all should speak of him as "His Eminence Death," which pleased nearly everyone.

Captain Compson, known both as England's most dashing cavalry officer and most elegant rake, remarked next, "That's all very well, but how is the invitation to reach Death? Does anyone here know where he lives?"

"Death undoubtedly lives in London," said Lady Neville, "like everyone else of any importance, though he probably goes to

Deauville for the summer. Actually, Death must live fairly near my own house. This is much the best section of London, and you could hardly expect a person of Death's importance to live anywhere else. When I stop to think of it, it's really rather strange that we haven't met before now, on the street."

Most of her friends agreed with her, but the poet, whose name was David Lorimond, cried out, "No, my lady, you are wrong! Death lives among the poor. Death lives in the foulest, darkest alleys of this city, in some vile, rat-ridden hovel that smells of—" He stopped here, partly because Lady Neville had indicated her displeasure, and partly because he had never been inside such a hut or thought of wondering what it smelled like. "Death lives among the poor," he went on, "and comes to visit them every day, for he is their only friend."

Lady Neville answered him as coldly as she had spoken to the young lord. "He may be forced to deal with them, David, but I hardly think that he seeks them out as companions. I am certain that it is as difficult for him to think of the poor as individuals as it is for me. Death is, after all, a nobleman."

There was no real argument among the lords and ladies that Death lived in a neighborhood at least as good as their own, but none of them seemed to know the name of Death's street, and no one had ever seen Death's house.

"If there were a war," Captain Compson said, "Death would be easy to find. I have seen him, you know, even spoken to him, but he has never answered me."

"Quite proper," said Lady Neville. "Death must always speak first. You are not a very correct person, Captain." But she smiled at him, as all women did.

Then an idea came to her. "My hairdresser has a sick child, I understand," she said. "He was telling me about it yesterday, sounding most dull and hopeless. I will send for him and give him the invitation, and he in his turn can give it to Death when he comes to take the brat. A bit unconventional, I admit, but I see no other way."

"If he refuses?" asked a lord who had just been married.

"Why should he?" asked Lady Neville.

Again it was the poet who exclaimed amidst the general approval that this was a cruel and wicked thing to do. But he fell silent when Lady Neville innocently asked him, "Why, David?"

So the hairdresser was sent for, and when he stood before them, smiling nervously and twisting his hands to be in the same room with so many great lords, Lady Neville told him the errand that was required of him. And she was right, as she usually was, for he made no refusal. He merely took the invitation in his hand and asked to be excused.

He did not return for two days, but when he did he presented himself to Lady Neville without being sent for and handed her a small white envelope. Saying, "How very nice of you, thank you very much," she opened it and found therein a plain calling card with nothing on it except these words: *Death will be pleased to attend Lady Neville's ball.*

"Death gave you this?" she asked the hairdresser eagerly. "What was he like?" But the hairdresser stood still, looking past her, and said nothing, and she, not really waiting for an answer, called a dozen servants to her and told them to run and summon her friends. As she paced up and down the room waiting for them, she asked again, "What is Death like?" The hairdresser did not reply.

When her friends came they passed the little card excitedly from hand to hand, until it had gotten quite smudged and bent from their fingers. But they all admitted that, beyond its message, there was nothing particularly unusual about it. It was neither hot nor cold to the touch, and what little odor clung to it was rather pleasant. Everyone said that it was a very familiar smell, but no one could give it a name. The poet said that it reminded him of lilacs but not exactly.

It was Captain Compson, however, who pointed out the one thing that no one else had noticed. "Look at the handwriting itself," he said. "Have you ever seen anything more graceful? The letters seem as light as birds. I think we have wasted our time speaking of Death as His This and His That. A woman wrote this note."

Then there was an uproar and a great babble, and the card had to be handed around again so that everyone could exclaim, "Yes, by God!" over it. The voice of the poet rose out of the hubbub saying, "It is very natural, when you come to think of it. After all, the French say *la mort*. Lady Death. I should much prefer Death to be a woman."

"Death rides a great black horse," said Captain Compson firmly, "and wears armor of the same color. Death is very tall, taller than anyone. It was no woman I saw on the battlefield, striking right and left like any soldier. Perhaps the hairdresser wrote it himself, or the hairdresser's wife."

But the hairdresser refused to speak, though they gathered around him and begged him to say who had given him the note. At first they promised him all sorts of rewards, and later they threatened to do terrible things to him. "Did you write this card?" he was asked, and "Who wrote it, then? Was it a living woman? Was it really Death? Did Death say anything to you? How did you know it was Death? Is Death a woman? Are you trying to make fools of us all?"

Not a word from the hairdresser, not one word, and finally Lady Neville called her servants to have him whipped and thrown into the street. He did not look at her as they took him away, or utter a sound.

Silencing her friends with a wave of her hand, Lady Neville said, "The ball will take place two weeks from tonight. Let Death come as Death pleases, whether as man or woman or strange, sexless creature." She smiled calmly. "Death may well be a woman," she said. "I am less certain of Death's form than I was, but I am also less frightened of Death. I am too old to be afraid of anything that can use a quill pen to write me a letter. Go home now, and as you make your preparations for the ball see that you speak of it to your servants, that they may spread the news all over London. Let it be known that on this one night no one in the world will die, for Death will be dancing at Lady Neville's ball."

For the next two weeks Lady Neville's great house shook and groaned and creaked like an old tree in a gale as the servants hammered and scrubbed, polished and painted making ready for the ball. Lady Neville had always been very proud of her house, but as the ball drew near she began to be afraid that it would not be nearly grand enough for Death, who was surely accustomed to visiting in the homes of richer, mightier people than herself. Fearing the scorn of Death, she worked night and day supervising her servants' preparations. Curtains and carpets had to be cleaned, goldwork and silverware polished until they gleamed by themselves in the dark. The grand staircase that rushed down into the ballroom like a waterfall was washed and rubbed so often that it was almost impossible to walk on it without slipping. As for the ballroom itself, it took thirty-two servants working at once to clean it properly, not counting those who were polishing the glass chandelier that was taller than a man and the fourteen smaller lamps. And when they were done she made them do it all over, not because she saw any dust or dirt anywhere, but because she was sure that Death would.

As for herself, she chose her finest gown and saw to its laundering personally. She called in another hairdresser and had him put up her hair in the style of an earlier time, wanting to show Death that she was a woman who enjoyed her age and did not find it necessary to ape the young and beautiful. All the day of the ball she sat before her mirror, not making herself up much beyond the normal touches of rouge and eye shadow and fine rice powder, but staring at the lean old face she had been born with, wondering how it would appear to Death. Her steward asked her to approve his wine selection, but she sent him away and stayed at her mirror until it was time to dress and go downstairs to meet her guests.

Everyone arrived early. When she looked out of a window, Lady Neville saw that the driveway of her home was choked with carriages and fine horses. "It all looks like a great funeral procession," she said. The footman cried the names of her guests to the echoing ballroom. "Captain Henry Compson. His Majesty's Household Cavalry! Mr. David Lorimond! Lord and Lady Torrance!!" (They were the youngest couple there, having been married only three months before.) "Sir Roger Harbison! The Contessa della Candini!" Lady Neville permitted them all to kiss her hand and made them welcome.

She had engaged the finest musicians she could find to play for the dancing, but though they began to play at her signal not one couple stepped out on the floor, nor did one young lord approach her to request the honor of the first dance, as was proper. They milled together, shining and murmuring, their eyes fixed on the ballroom door. Every time they heard a carriage clatter up the driveway they seemed to flinch a little and draw closer together; every time the footman announced the arrival of another guest, they all sighed softly and swayed a little on their feet with relief.

"Why did they come to my party if they were afraid?" Lady Neville muttered scornfully to herself. "I am not afraid of meeting Death. I ask only that Death may be impressed by the magnificence of my house and the flavor of my wines. I will die sooner than anyone here, but I am not afraid."

Certain that Death would not arrive until midnight, she moved among her guests, attempting to calm them, not with her words, which she knew they would not hear, but with the tone of her voice as if they were so many frightened horses. But little by little, she herself was infected by their nervousness: whenever she sat down she stood up again immediately, she tasted a dozen glasses of wine without finishing any of them, and she glanced constantly at her jeweled watch, at first wanting to hurry the midnight along and end the waiting, later scratching at the watch face with her forefinger, as if she would push away the night and drag the sun backward into the sky. When midnight came, she was standing with the rest of them, breathing through her mouth, shifting from foot to foot, listening for the sound of carriage wheels turning in gravel.

When the clock began to strike midnight, everyone, even Lady Neville and the brave Captain Compson, gave one startled little cry and then was silent again, listening to the tolling of the clock. The smaller clocks upstairs began to chime. Lady Neville's ears hurt. She caught sight of herself in the ballroom mirror, one gray face turned up toward the ceiling as if she were gasping for air, and she thought, "Death will be a woman, a hideous, filthy old crone as tall and strong as a man. And the most terrible thing of all will be that she will have my face." All the clocks stopped striking, and Lady Neville closed her eyes.

She opened them again only when she heard the whispering around her take on a different tone, one in which fear was fused with relief and a certain chagrin. For no new carriage stood in the driveway. Death had not come.

The noise grew slowly louder; here and there people were beginning to laugh. Near her, Lady Neville heard young Lord Torrance say to his wife, "There, my darling, I told you there was nothing to be afraid of. It was all a joke."

"I am ruined," Lady Neville thought. The laughter was increasing; it pounded against her ears in strokes, like the chiming of the clocks. "I wanted to give a ball so grand that those who were not invited would be shamed in front of the whole city, and this is my reward. I am ruined, and I deserve it."

Turning to the poet Lorimond, she said, "Dance with me, David." She signaled to the musicians, who at once began to play. When Lorimond hesitated, she said, "Dance with me now. You will not have another chance. I shall never give a party again."

Lorimond bowed and led her out onto the dance floor. The guests parted for them, and the laughter died down for a moment, but Lady Neville knew that it would soon begin again. "Well, let them laugh," she thought. "I did not fear Death when they were all trembling. Why should I fear their laughter?" But she could feel a stinging at the thin lids of her eyes, and she closed them once more as she began to dance with Lorimond.

And then, quite suddenly, all the carriage horses outside the house whinnied loudly, just once, as the guests had cried out at midnight. There were a great many horses, and their one salute was so loud that everyone in the room became instantly silent. They heard the heavy steps of the footman as he went to open the door, and they shivered as if they felt the cool breeze that drifted into the house. Then they heard a light voice saying, "Am I late? Oh. I am so sorry. The horses were tired," and before the footman could re-enter to announce her, a lovely young girl in a white dress stepped gracefully into the ballroom doorway and stood there smiling.

She could not have been more than nineteen. Her hair was yellow, and she wore it long. It fell thickly upon her bare shoulders that gleamed warmly through it, two limestone islands rising out of a dark golden sea. Her face was wide at the forehead and cheekbones, and narrow at the chin, and her skin was so clear that many of the ladies there—Lady Neville among them—touched their own faces wonderingly, and instantly drew their hands away as though their own skin had rasped their fingers. Her mouth was pale, where the mouths of other women were red and orange and even purple. Her eyebrows, thicker and straighter than was fashionable, met over dark, calm eyes that were set so deep in her young face and were so black, so uncompromisingly black, that the middle-aged wife of a middle-aged lord murmured, "Touch of the gypsy there, I think."

"Or something worse," suggested her husband's mistress.

"Be silent!" Lady Neville spoke louder than she had intended, and the girl turned to look at her. She smiled, and Lady Neville tried to smile back, but her mouth seemed very stiff. "Welcome," she said. "Welcome, my lady Death."

A sigh rustled among the lords and ladies as the girl took the old woman's hand and curtsied to her, sinking and rising in one motion, like a wave. "You are Lady Neville," she said. "Thank you so much for inviting me." Her accent was as faint and as almost familiar as her perfume.

"Please excuse me for being late," she said earnestly. "I had to come from a long way off, and my horses are so tired."

"The groom will rub them down," Lady Neville said, "and feed them if you wish."

"Oh, no," the girl answered quickly. "Tell him not to go near the horses, please. They are not really horses, and they are very fierce."

She accepted a glass of wine from a servant and drank it slowly, sighing softly and contentedly. "What good wine," she said. "And what a beautiful house you have."

"Thank you," said Lady Neville. Without turning, she could feel every woman in the room envying her, sensing it as she could always sense the approach of rain.

"I wish I lived here," Death said in her low, sweet voice. "I will, one day."

Then, seeing Lady Neville become as still as if she had turned to ice, she put her hand on the old woman's arm and said, "Oh, I'm sorry, I'm so sorry. I am so cruel, but I never mean to be. Please forgive me, Lady Neville. I am not used to company, and I do such stupid things. Please forgive me."

Her hand felt as light and warm on Lady Neville's arm as the hand of any other young girl, and her eyes were so appealing that Lady Neville replied, "You have said nothing wrong. While you are my guest, my house is yours."

"Thank you," said Death, and she smiled so radiantly that the musicians began to play quite by themselves, with no sign from Lady Neville. She would have stopped them, but Death said, "Oh, what lovely music! Let them play, please."

So the musicians played a gavotte, and Death, unabashed by eyes that stared at her in greedy terror, sang softly to herself without words, lifted her white gown slightly with both hands, and made hesitant little patting steps with her small feet. "I have not danced in so long," she said wistfully. "I'm quite sure I've forgotten how."

She was shy: she would not look up to embarrass the young lords, not one of whom stepped forward to dance with her. Lady Neville felt a flood of shame and sympathy, emotions she thought had withered in her years ago. "Is she to be humiliated at my own ball?" she thought angrily. "It is because she is Death; if she were the ugliest, foulest hag in all the world they would clamor to dance with her, because they are gentlemen and they know what is expected of them. But no gentleman will dance with Death, no matter how beautiful she is." She glanced sideways at David Lorimond. His face was flushed, and his hands were clasped so tightly as he stared at Death that his fingers were like glass, but when Lady Neville touched his arm he did not turn, and when she hissed, "David!", he pretended not to hear her.

Then Captain Compson, gray-haired and handsome in his uniform, stepped out of the crowd and bowed gracefully before Death. "If I may have the honor," he said.

"Captain Compson," said Death, smiling. She put her arm in his. "I was hoping you would ask me."

This brought a frown from the older women, who did not consider it a proper thing to say, but for that Death cared not a rap. Captain Compson led her to the center of the floor, and there they danced. Death was curiously graceless at first—she was too anxious to please her partner, and she seemed to have no notion of rhythm. The Captain himself moved with the mixture of dignity and humor that Lady Neville had never seen in another man, but when he looked at her over Death's shoulder, she saw something that no one else appeared to notice: that his face and eyes were immobile with fear, and that, though he offered Death his hand with easy gallantry, he flinched slightly when she took it. And yet he danced as well as Lady Neville had ever seen him.

"Ah, that's what comes of having a reputation to maintain," she thought. "Captain Compson too must do what is expected of him. I hope someone else will dance with her soon."

But no one did. Little by little, other couples overcame their fear and slipped hurriedly out on the floor when Death was looking the other way, but nobody sought to relieve Captain Compson of his beautiful partner. They danced every dance together. In time, some of the men present began to look at her with more appreciation than terror, but when she returned their glances and smiled at them, they clung to their partners as if a cold wind were threatening to blow them away.

One of the few who stared at her frankly and with pleasure was young Lord Torrance, who usually danced only with his wife. Another was the poet Lorimond. Dancing with Lady Neville, he remarked to her, "If she is Death, what do these frightened fools think they are? If she is ugliness, what must they be? I hate their fear. It is obscene."

Death and the Captain danced past them at that moment, and they heard him say to her, "But if that was truly you that I saw in the battle, how can you have changed so? How can you have become so lovely?"

Death's laughter was gay and soft. "I thought that among so

many beautiful people it might be better to be beautiful. I was afraid of frightening everyone and spoiling the party."

"They all thought she would be ugly," said Lorimond to Lady Neville. "I—I knew she would be beautiful."

"Then why have you not danced with her?" Lady Neville asked him. "Are you also afraid?"

"No, oh, no," the poet answered quickly and passionately. "I will ask her to dance very soon. I only want to look at her a little longer."

The musicians played on and on. The dancing wore away the night as slowly as falling water wears down a cliff. It seemed to Lady Neville that no night had ever endured longer, and yet she was neither tired nor bored. She danced with every man there, except with Lord Torrance, who was dancing with his wife as if they had just met that night, and, of course, with Captain Compson. Once he lifted his hand and touched Death's golden hair very lightly. He was a striking man still, a fit partner for so beautiful a girl, but Lady Neville looked at his face each time she passed him and realized that he was older than anyone knew.

Death herself seemed younger than the youngest there. No woman at the ball danced better than she now, though it was hard for Lady Neville to remember at what point her awkwardness had given way to the liquid sweetness of her movements. She smiled and called to everyone who caught her eye—and she knew them all by name; she sang constantly, making up words to the dance tunes, nonsense words, sounds without meaning, and yet everyone strained to hear her soft voice without knowing why. And when, during a waltz, she caught up the trailing end of her gown to give her more freedom as she danced, she seemed to Lady Neville to move like a little sailing boat over a still evening sea.

Lady Neville heard Lady Torrance arguing angrily with the Contessa della Candini. "I don't care if she is Death, she's no older than I am, she can't be!"

"Nonsense," said the Contessa, who could not afford to be generous to any other woman. "She is twenty-eight, thirty, if she is an hour. And that dress, that bridal gown she wears—really!"

"Vile," said the woman who had come to the ball as Captain Compson's freely acknowledged mistress. "Tasteless. But one should know better than to expect taste from Death, I suppose." Lady Torrance looked as if she were going to cry.

"They are jealous of Death," Lady Neville said to herself.

"How strange. I am not jealous of her, not in the least. And I do not fear her at all." She was very proud of herself.

Then, as unbiddenly as they had begun to play, the musicians stopped. They began to put away their instruments. In the sudden shrill silence, Death pulled away from Captain Compson and ran to look out of one of the tall windows, pushing the curtains apart with both hands. "Look!" she said, with her back turned to them. "Come and look. The night is almost gone."

The summer sky was still dark, and the eastern horizon was only a shade lighter than the rest of the sky, but the stars had vanished and the trees near the house were gradually becoming distinct. Death pressed her face against the window and said, so softly that the other guests could barely hear her, "I must go now."

"No," Lady Neville said, and was not immediately aware that she had spoken. "You must stay a while longer. The ball was in your honor. Please stay."

Death held out both hands to her, and Lady Neville came and took them in her own. "I've had a wonderful time," she said gently. "You cannot possibly imagine how it feels to be actually invited to such a ball as this, because you have given them and gone to them all your life. One is like another to you, but for me it is different. Do you understand me?" Lady Neville nodded silently. "I will remember this night forever," Death said.

"Stay," Captain Compson said. "Stay just a little longer." He put his hand on Death's shoulder, and she smiled and leaned her cheek against it. "Dear Captain Compson," she said. "My first real gallant. Aren't you tired of me yet?"

"Never," he said. "Please stay."

"Stay," said Lorimond, and he too seemed about to touch her. "Stay. I want to talk to you. I want to look at you. I will dance with you if you stay."

"How many followers I have," Death said in wonder. She stretched one hand toward Lorimond, but he drew back from her and then flushed in shame. "A soldier and a poet. How wonderful it is to be a woman. But why did you not speak to me earlier, both of you? Now it is too late. I must go."

"Please, stay," Lady Torrance whispered. She held on to her husband's hand for courage. "We think you are so beautiful, both of us do."

"Gracious Lady Torrance," the girl said kindly. She turned back to the window, touched it lightly, and it flew open. The cool dawn air rushed into the ballroom, fresh with rain but already smelling faintly of the London streets over which it had passed. They heard birdsong and the strange, harsh nickering of Death's horses.

"Do you want me to stay?" she asked. The question was put, not to Lady Neville, nor to Captain Compson, nor to any of her admirers, but to the Contessa della Candini, who stood well back from them all, hugging her flowers to herself and humming a little song of irritation. She did not in the least want Death to stay, but she was afraid that all the other women would think her envious of Death's beauty, and so she said, "Yes. Of course I do."

"Ah," said Death. She was almost whispering. "And you," she said to another woman, "do you want me to stay? Do you want me to be one of your friends?"

"Yes," said the woman, "because you are beautiful and a true lady."

"And you," said Death to a man, "and you," to a woman, "and you," to another man, "do you want me to stay?" And they all answered, "Yes, Lady Death, we do."

"Do you want me, then?" she cried at last to all of them. "Do you want me to live among you and to be one of you, and not to be Death anymore? Do you want me to visit your houses and come to all your parties? Do you want me to ride horses like yours instead of mine, do you want me to wear the kind of dresses you wear, and say the things you would say? Would one of you marry me, and would the rest of you dance at my wedding and bring gifts to my children? Is that what you want?"

"Yes," said Lady Neville. "Stay here, stay with me, stay with us."

Death's voice, without becoming louder, had become clearer and older; too old a voice, thought Lady Neville, for such a young girl. "Be sure," said Death. "Be sure of what you want, be very sure. Do all of you want me to stay? For if one of you says to me, no, go away, then I must leave at once and never return. Be sure. Do you all want me?"

And everyone there cried with one voice, "Yes! Yes, you must stay with us. You are so beautiful that we cannot let you go."

"We are tired," said Captain Compson.

"We are blind," said Lorimond, adding, "especially to poetry."

"We are afraid," said Lord Torrance quietly, and his wife took his arm and said, "Both of us."

"We are dull and stupid," said Lady Neville, "and growing old uselessly. Stay with us, Lady Death."

And then Death smiled sweetly and radiantly and took a step forward, and it was as though she had come down among them from a great height. "Very well," she said. "I will stay with you. I will be Death no more. I will be a woman."

The room was full of a deep sigh, although no one was seen to open his mouth. No one moved, for the golden-haired girl was Death still, and her horses still whinnied for her outside. No one could look at her for long, although she was the most beautiful girl anyone there had ever seen.

"There is a price to pay," she said. "There is always a price. Some one of you must become Death in my place, for there must forever be Death in the world. Will anyone choose? Will anyone here become Death of his own free will? For only thus can I become a human girl."

No one spoke, no one spoke at all. But they backed slowly away from her, like waves slipping back down a beach to the sea when you try to catch them. The Contessa della Candini and her friends would have crept quietly out of the door, but Death smiled at them and they stood where they were. Captain Compson opened his mouth as though he were going to declare himself, but he said nothing. Lady Neville did not move.

"No one," said Death. She touched a flower with her finger, and it seemed to crouch and flex itself like a pleased cat. "No one at all," she said. "Then I must choose, and that is just, for that is the way that I became Death. I never wanted to be Death, and it makes me so happy that you want me to become one of yourselves. I have searched a long time for people who would want me. Now I have only to choose someone to replace me and it is done. I will choose very carefully."

"Oh, we were so foolish," Lady Neville said to herself. "We were so foolish." But she said nothing aloud; she merely clapped her hands and stared at the young girl thinking vaguely that if she had had a daughter she would have been greatly pleased if she resembled the lady Death.

"The Contessa della Candini," said Death thoughtfully, and that woman gave a little squeak of terror because she could not draw her breath for a scream. But Death laughed and said, "No, that would be silly." She said nothing more, but for a long time after that the Contessa burned with humiliation at not having been chosen to be Death.

"Not Captain Compson," murmured Death, "because he is too

kind to become Death, and because it would be too cruel to him. He wants to die so badly." The expression on the Captain's face did not change, but his hands began to tremble.

"Not Lorimond," the girl continued, "because he knows so little about life, and because I like him." The poet flushed, and turned white, and then turned pink again. He made as if to kneel clumsily on one knee, but instead he pulled himself erect and stood as much like Captain Compson as he could.

"Not the Torrances," said Death, "never Lord and Lady Torrance for both of them care too much about another person to take any pride in being Death." But she hesitated over Lady Torrance for a while, staring at her out of her dark and curious eyes. "I was your age when I became Death," she said at last. "I wonder what it will be like to be your age again. I have been Death for so long." Lady Torrance shivered and did not speak.

And at last Death said quietly, "Lady Neville."

"I am here," Lady Neville answered.

"I think you are the only one," said Death. "I choose you, Lady Neville."

Again Lady Neville heard every guest sigh softly, and although her back was to them all she knew that they were sighing in relief that neither themselves nor anyone dear to themselves had been chosen. Lady Torrance gave a little cry of protest, but Lady Neville knew that she would have cried out at whatever choice Death made. She heard herself say calmly, "I am honored. But was there no one more worthy than I?"

"Not one," said Death. "There is no one quite so weary of being human, no one who knows better how meaningless it is to be alive. And there is no one else here with the power to treat life"—and she smiled sweetly and cruelly—"the life of your hairdresser's child, for instance, as the meaningless thing it is. Death has a heart, but it is forever an empty heart, and I think, Lady Neville, that your heart is like a dry riverbed, like a seashell. You will be very content as Death, more so than I, for I was very young when I became Death."

She came toward Lady Neville, light and swaying, her deep eyes wide and full of the light of the red morning sun that was beginning to rise. The guests at the ball moved back from her, although she did not look at them, but Lady Neville clenched her hands tightly and watched Death come toward her with her little dancing steps. "We must kiss each other," Death said. "That is the way I became Death." She shook her head delightedly, so that her soft hair swirled about her shoulders. "Quickly, quickly," she said. "Oh, I cannot wait to be human again."

"You may not like it," Lady Neville said. She felt very calm, though she could hear her old heart pounding in her chest and feel it in the tips of her fingers. "You may not like it after a while," she said.

"Perhaps not." Death's smile was very close to her now. "I will not be as beautiful as I am, and perhaps people will not love me as much as they do now. But I will be human for a while, and at last I will die. I have done my penance."

"What penance?" the old woman asked the beautiful girl. "What was it you did? Why did you become Death?"

"I don't remember," said the lady Death. "And you too will forget in time." She was smaller than Lady Neville and so much younger. In her white dress she might have been the daughter that Lady Neville had never had, who would have been with her always and held her mother's head lightly in the crook of her arm when she felt old and sad. Now she lifted her head to kiss Lady Neville's cheek, and as she did so she whispered in her ear, "You will still be beautiful when I am ugly. Be kind to me then."

Behind Lady Neville the handsome gentlemen and ladies murmured and sighed, fluttering like moths in their evening dress in their elegant gowns. "I promise," she said, and then she pursed her dry lips to kiss the soft, sweet-smelling cheek of the young lady Death.

RESPONSE

1. What does Lady Neville hope to gain by asking Death to her party?

2. Why does the hairdresser refuse to talk about Death?

3. Comment on the appropriateness of the manifestation of death as a young woman.

4. Why is Lady Neville chosen over the other characters in the story to be Death?

EXTENSION

5. Imagine you are one of the guests at the party. Describe in detail what occurred when Lady Neville kissed the cheek of the young lady Death.

Loving

May Your First Love Be Your Last

Gregory Clark

> Have you ever been afraid to introduce yourself to someone you really wanted to know? How did you finally arrange to meet this person?
>
> Do you believe in love at first sight? Explain.

By and large, I have had little trouble with the fair sex. I mean, of course, that they have troubled little with me.

Being the first-born of my family, I was naturally a Mamma's Boy. By the time I was five, I already realized, dimly, my responsibility to demonstrate to the younger members of the family, arriving, how to behave. By the time I was eight, I did not have to be told about Tuesdays and Fridays. On Tuesdays and Fridays I put out the ash cans and garbage cans as a matter of course. I wrestled them out to the curb, though I was a shrimp, or whiffet (as we small ones were called). By the age of ten my senses were so acute that at six o'clock in the morning, I could hear the soft snowflakes beating upon the attic bedroom window. Softly I would rise. Softly I would dress, waking neither my young brother and sister, nor my parents. And the first shovel you heard on Howland avenue, at 7 a.m., was mine. All the mothers of Howland avenue admired me.

They pointed me out as a model to their sons. And I was beaten up as a matter of course and frequently had a bloody nose. I was an object of contempt to my generation.

By the time I was twelve, I was so covered with freckles—face, shoulders, arms, hands—that you could hardly see me. From amidst the freckles, my piggy blue eyes looked out eagerly. But nobody looked back. Especially the fair sex. I was spared those grim years of adolescence. No girls troubled me.

Now, do not think I was lonely. Forlorn? Well, maybe a little; but we all must feel forlorn one time or another in our lives. Fortunately, on the next street, Albany avenue, lived two older boys named Hoyes Lloyd and Stuart Thompson who became in their time two of the greatest field naturalists of Canada. They were glad of a queue of younger boys to follow them in their bird watching, tree naming, plant identifying, butterfly knowing, beetle picking, stone recognizing. And thus I escaped the clutches of the fair sex through those perilous years, thirteen to nineteen. Freckles do it. I became bewitched by the lovely elusive world of nature. And it has remained my love for more than sixty years.

But now I come to the point where I must tell the truth, the whole truth, and nothing but the truth, so help me!

I had fallen in love at the age of thirteen.

She was eleven.

To this day, I can show you the fire hydrant beside the Royal Conservatory of Music in Toronto where I dropped my four public library books and pretended to tie my shoelace.

I watched them go by.

She was being dragged along by an older big blonde sister named Beth (as I later found out) but she was small and dark, with the most beautiful great eyes I ever saw or have ever seen. As she swept past, she looked at me. But she did not see me. (As I later found out.)

As a matter of fact, she did not see me for seven long years.

But, oh, I saw her.

They turned into Orde street, which was the first street down University avenue behind the Conservatory. Quick as a weasel, I snatched up my books and followed. Orde street is gone now, a blind street off University; tall skyscrapers loom. The old houses are all gone. But when I nipped around the corner, I saw the two of them scamper up the front steps of one house. And I could tell they were home.

I walked past the house. No. 6 Orde street. When I was safely out of its sight, I flew. Like a swallow, I flew up and along College street, up St. George, along Bloor street to the drug store of Mr. Norris at the corner of Howland. He was my friend. He also had a fat yellow book called a City Directory. Breathlessly, I told Mr. Norris of my need to know who lived at 6 Orde street. He was a perceptive man.

"Reverend James Murray," he said, looking in the Directory.

After a moment's reflection, and having no doubt been thirteen years old himself once, he then took the skimpy telephone book of that time and looked up Reverend James Murray.

"College 608," he said to central when she answered. (Though this was sixty years ago, I still remember that number.)

"Pardon me, ma'am," said Mr. Norris when someone answered. "But at what church does the Reverend Mr. Murray officiate? Erskine Presbyterian? Thank you."

And hung up.

"Erskine Presbyterian," Mr. Norris informed me with a smile I like to think I remember too.

Ah, well, from there on it is just the usual story. I had to go to Bloor street Presbyterian Church with my family at the morning service. But each Sunday evening, I was in the balcony of Erskine Church. This in time gave rise, by the time I was sixteen, to the general belief in my family and their friends that I was intending to enter the Presbyterian ministry. And they were all very pleased.

Year after year, every Sunday evening, I sat and watched. Oh, sometimes I would lose heart. Especially when, the moment the service ended, I would hastily skip down and mingle with the crowd that always gathered outside for a little while. And I would see her. She never saw me, I think now that if she had looked at me, I would have collapsed into a blob of jelly on the pavement. But what tormented me was that she grew more beautiful every year, far beyond my wildest reach of hope.

When I was seventeen or eighteen and started to Varsity, I was old enough to realize my folly, and for weeks I would not go to Erskine Church. But then, like a dog, I would creep back. Never had I heard her voice. So in my dreams I gave her a soft, contralto voice. Never had I seen her teeth, for she was a Presbyterian Murray who did not go about smiling in all directions. So I gave her beautiful white teeth. I gave her a character gentle, serene, compassionate. She was so perfect, by the time I was finished with her, that at the age of twenty, having had one last fearful look at her in the outpouring crowd of Erskine Church, I abandoned all hope, all dreams.

On the 17th of January, 1913, age twenty, I was a cub reporter on a newspaper. The University had thrown me out when I failed the first year twice, due to my devotion to the University newspaper, *The Varsity*. Each Friday, at 3 p.m., the staff of my new employers could draw their salaries. Mine was $12 a week. With this, around 4:30 in the afternoon, I would proceed to the Little Blue Tea Room on Yonge street, up a flight of stairs. There I would generously entertain my erstwhile Varsity friends to tea and cinnamon toast, or crumpets, or cocoa in winter. With about $3 I could play host in high style.

At 4:30 of January 17 I walked up the stairs and into the tea room. There were numbers of people sitting at the different tables. I headed for the alcove which was reserved for our Varsity party.

"Greg," said a young man whose name I have forgotten, rising to beckon me.

There was a girl with her back to me at his table.

"I'd like to introduce . . . " he began.

It was like being struck by lightning.

She smiled with the lips and teeth I had given her. At close range, she was more beautiful than I had painted her in my most magical dreams.

I took her home that afternoon. And no man ever took her home again. I was invited to supper. Reverend Mr. Murray, who was a tall, dark handsome man, looked at me with an expression I had long been familiar with in the passing brief glances of people. He told me long afterwards that on that first occasion he thought I was the dullest young man he had ever encountered.

I wasn't dull! I just wasn't THERE. I was in the Seventh Heaven, where no one speaks. The big blonde sister Beth whom first I had seen seven years before dragging my love along by the hand tried to monopolize the conversation at the supper table. But Mr. Murray and my love talked about fishing in Nova Scotia, and how the reverend gentleman had taught his little dark daughter to cast trout flies.

That was ONE thing I did not design for her. But when I heard about the trout fishing, I knew she was mine.

We were engaged six months later. We were married on the eve of the day before I sailed overseas to be absent from her two and a half years of war. For all but three years of half a century, we lived a joyous life, with only the one great tragedy when our first-born son was killed in battle in the second war. She died in my arms.

But you see I was possessed. That is why the fair sex have not bothered with me. They must sense when they see a man possessed.

Now why, you may ask, on this wintry night, do I tell so secret and idle a tale as this?

Well, on a wintry night such as this, the young, the ones on the threshold of life, are likely to be at home on a Saturday night. And on a Saturday, *Weekend Magazine* comes in. Maybe more often than at other times, the young, on the threshold of thirteen, fourteen, are more likely to come upon this story.

I tell you what you do, boy. Or girl.

Go and look at the western sky where the new moon, the silver shaving of the moon, hangs.

Look at it over your LEFT shoulder, and wish.

Wish that your first love shall be your last love.

And if your wish is granted, you will have put on the whole armour of life.

RESPONSE

1. What do you think of Clark's behaviour as a teenage boy in love?

2. Select those passages from Clark's story that suggest he was "possessed."

3. If you were the young woman in "May Your First Love Be Your Last," would you welcome the kind of attention she receives? Explain.

4. Why do you think Gregory Clark's wish for you is that your first love be your last?

EXTENSION

5. Write an account of the beginning of this relationship from the young woman's point of view.

6. Compose a dialogue between the girl and her father which might have occurred after the first dinner with Clark.

The Tender Trap

Mary Kay Blakely

> Does the behaviour of friends of the same sex change in the company of members of the opposite sex? How does this behaviour make you feel? What generates these feelings?

I was still in that fuzzy, post-party fog when I picked up the phone—it was the morning after the bacchanalian, hilarious, affectionate celebration my friends had staged for my 40th birthday. So it took me a few minutes to register the TV producer's urgency when she asked me to cancel my plans for the next Tuesday, travel to New York, and debate Dr. Toni Grant on a national talk show.

"Who is he?" I asked, suppressing a yawn.

"She," the producer said impatiently, "is a psychologist and the author of a new book: *Being a Woman—Fulfilling Your Femininity and Finding Love*. It's getting a *lot* of media attention." I was less than amazed to learn that media hearts were pumping again over another book about women and love, given the tremendous amount of ink poured over women who love too much, not enough, make foolish choices, or love men who hate them. With the possible exception of reshaping women's thighs, there is almost no cause approached more devotedly than straightening out the inept, misguided, unsatisfying way women love men.

Dr. Grant's theory is that the Women's Movement did us in by cultivating ambition and assertiveness, in direct collision with male expectations of submission and deference. Women suffer loveless lives, she proposed, because they'd swallowed "the 10 big lies of liberation." The producer suggested it was my duty, presumably as a woman who'd swallowed the lies and survived, to challenge

Dr. Grant on live TV. She thought I'd be a sporting opponent to the psychologist's theory that "it's better to be loved than to be right."

I promised her I'd think about it and call her back.

And I *did* think about it, despite a recent vow to swear off all such invitations. "Do you know what you do wrong on talk shows?" a friend calling with an impromptu critique had asked after my last appearance. "You really try to *talk*. Nobody's interested in real conversation at six-thirty a.m.—they're interested in entertainment." I remembered the debates I've had over the last 10 years with outrageous chauvinists and totaled women, serving as foil to any irresponsible idea about women a producer decided to telecast. My friend was right: my passion for women's rights aired as entertainment.

Weighing my plans for Tuesday against contributing my two cents to a debate on whether it's better to be loved or to be right, I declined the invitation. How did I feel, shirking my duty to millions of viewers who would be exposed to Dr. Grant's denigrating advice? Fine.

If the new theory achieves a temporary popularity, it won't be the first or last time women were sold down the river of love. In the desperate search for lasting relationships, women have been persuaded to bundle themselves in Saran Wrap, to express rage silently by flinging cotton balls at their bathroom mirrors, and never, never, to criticize their man. There undoubtedly will be some enthusiasm for Dr. Grant's formula, at least initially, from women who are weary of being right and feeling unloved.

I suspect the weariness is widespread, because last night someone made reference to a scene in the film *Broadcast News*. When the ambitious, idealistic journalist, fully aware that her male boss prefers acquiescent women, challenges him on a decision they both knew was wrong, he responds by attempting to humiliate her: "It must be a terrible burden to be right all the time," he says sarcastically. "Yes," she says, unhumbled. "It is." There was enormous identification with that remark among friends who felt similarly burdened. They would rather not be right, rather not have to push for change. They would rather have things already changed. Yet they continue to carry the burden. Why, when they know as well as Dr. Grant that men have a harder time loving women who challenge them?

It was a question that most of the guests at my 40th-birthday party had answered at some point in their lives. We were long past the first blush of adolescent love, when the desire to be loved dominated the need to be who we were. All of us, I suppose, had faked a kind of lovableness in our youth, by abandoning the complicated parts of ourselves that threatened first bliss. If we could have stopped time, remained in adolescence, we might have continued this pleasantly faked happiness. But buried ambitions or deeply felt beliefs, simmering over time, eventually create heat. It was no longer satisfying to be loved without revealing who we really were. There's an untellable loneliness in being drenched with love directed at someone else.

To suggest love means never having to say you're right is bad advice for teenagers, but it's impossible advice for grown women. It's unimaginable that the wise, thoughtful, witty women at my 40th-birthday party—who've paid heavy dues in their lifetimes to discover who they are—would be more lovable if they stifled the complex or demanding parts of themselves. In fact, it's embarrassing to be known in this group as a two-personality woman, irresolutely stuck between stages of evolution.

Perhaps that is the population Dr. Grant has in mind as her audience—women who present one self to women but another to men. I watched a dramatic example of such chameleonlike behavior at a meeting recently, when a knowledgeable, forceful, intelligent businesswoman was reduced to a solicitous, indecisive, giggling incompetent the moment a single man entered the room. Her colleagues blushed for her.

Could the man have felt flattered by her reduction? The ratio at my 40th-birthday party—20 women to three men—suggests there is not a huge population of grown men comfortable with grown women. There are plenty of books by male authors, nostalgic for the good old days when women stifled themselves. Change takes time, as the media are fond of reporting. But for those few men who have ventured out of the territory of adolescent love into the rich frontiers of deeper passions, there seems to be a holding attraction. I saw that, too, on the mature faces of two of the partyers last night.

This man had been in love for nearly a decade with a woman heavily burdened with "being right." Together, they'd swallowed every one of the "big lies" of liberation Dr. Grant mentions in her book—they'd argued about housework, took turns accommodating the moves of two full-blown careers, examined their parenting responsibilities in excruciating detail. Thousands of episodes concerning "who's right" had passed between them, providing each with a thorough, unabridged version of who they were.

They were standing on opposite sides of the room when he caught her eye and, without needing to interrupt her animated conversation, deftly delivered a solidly affectionate, peculiarly intimate smile. There are no shortcuts to that rare smile passing uncoyly between genders—it took this man and woman 40 years and millions of words to earn it. But it gave me goose bumps as I recognized it flashing across the room, that bolt of affection electrified by respect. Here was a woman thoroughly loved precisely because she had risked being right.

RESPONSE

1. Do you agree with Dr. Grant's contention that "it's better to be loved than to be right"? Explain.

2. Do you agree with Dr. Grant's opinion that "men have a harder time loving women who challenge them"? Explain.

3. How do Blakely's ideas differ from Dr. Grant's?

4. Using the ideas presented in Blakely's editorial, devise a point-form character sketch of the grown man.

5. Have you ever witnessed people in an intimate relationship disputing whose viewpoint is right? Do you find this behaviour appropriate? Explain.

EXTENSION

6. Write the dialogue that might take place between a man who expects a woman to be submissive and a woman who challenges his attempts to dominate her.

7. Explain why you agree or disagree with this statement: The educational system supports male dominance.

Gawain and The Lady Ragnell

Ethel Johnston Phelps

What is autonomy?

Is it possible for both partners to be autonomous in an enduring relationship?

Long ago, in the days of King Arthur, the finest knight in all Britain was the king's nephew Gawain. He was, by reputation, the bravest in battle, the wisest, the most courteous, the most compassionate, and the most loyal to his king.

One day in late summer, Gawain was with Arthur and the knights of the court at Carlisle in the north. The king returned from the day's hunting looking so pale and shaken that Gawain followed him at once to his chamber.

"What has happened, my lord?" asked Gawain with concern.

Arthur sat down heavily. "I had a very strange encounter in Inglewood Forest . . . I hardly know what to make of it." And he related to Gawain what had occurred.

"Today I hunted a great white stag," said Arthur. "The stag at last escaped me and I was alone, some distance from my men. Suddenly a tall, powerful man appeared before me with sword upraised."

"And you were unarmed!"

"Yes. I had only my bow and a dagger in my belt. He threatened to kill me," Arthur went on. "And he swung his sword as though he meant to cut me down on the spot! Then he laughed horribly and said he would give me one chance to save my life."

"Who was this man?" cried Gawain. "Why should he want to kill you?"

"He said his name was Sir Gromer, and he sought revenge for the loss of his northern lands."

"A chieftain from the north!" exclaimed Gawain. "But what is this one chance he spoke of?"

"I gave him my word I would meet him one year from to-day, unarmed, at the same spot, with the answer to a question!" said Arthur.

Gawain started to laugh, but stopped at once when he saw Arthur's face. "A question! Is it a riddle? And one year to find the answer? That should not be hard!"

"If I can bring him the true answer to the question, 'What is it that women most desire, above all else?' my life will be spared." Arthur scowled. "He is sure I will fail. It must be a foolish riddle that no one can answer."

"My lord, we have one year to search the kingdom for answers," said Gawain confidently. "I will help you. Surely one of the answers will be the right one."

"No doubt you are right—someone will know the answer." Arthur looked more cheerful. "The man is mad, but a chieftain will keep his word."

For the next twelve months, Arthur and Gawain asked the question from one corner of the kingdom to the other. Then at last the appointed day drew near. Although they had many answers, Arthur was worried.

"With so many answers to choose from, how do we know which is the right one?" he asked in despair. "Not one of them has the ring of truth."

A few days before he was to meet Sir Gromer, Arthur rode out alone through the golden gorse and purple heather. The track led upward toward a grove of great oaks. Arthur, deep in thought, did not look up until he reached the edge of the oak wood. When he raised his head, he pulled up suddenly in astonishment.

Before him was a grotesque woman. She was almost as wide as she was high, her skin was mottled green, and spikes of weedlike hair covered her head. Her face seemed more animal than human.

The woman's eyes met Arthur's fearlessly. "You are Arthur the king," she said in a harsh, croaking voice. "In two days time you must meet Sir Gromer with the answer to a question."

Arthur turned cold with fear. He stammered, "Yes . . . yes . . . that is true. Who are you? How did you know of this?"

"I am the lady Ragnell. Sir Gromer is my stepbrother. You haven't found the true answer, have you?"

"I have many answers," Arthur replied curtly. "I do not see

how my business concerns you." He gathered up the reins, eager to be gone.

"You do not have the right answer." Her certainty filled him with a sense of doom. The harsh voice went on, "But I know the answer to Sir Gromer's question."

Arthur turned back in hope and disbelief. "You do? Tell me the true answer to his question, and I will give you a large bag of gold."

"I have no use for gold," she said coldly.

"Nonsense, my good woman. With gold you can buy anything you want!" He hesitated a moment, for the huge, grotesque face with the cool, steady eyes unnerved him. He went on hurriedly, "What is it you want? Jewelry? Land? Whatever you want I will pay you—that is, if you truly have the right answer."

"I know the answer. I promise you that!" She paused. "What I demand in return is that the knight Gawain become my husband."

There was a moment of shocked silence. Then Arthur cried, "Impossible! You ask the impossible, woman!"

She shrugged and turned to leave.

"Wait, wait a moment!" Rage and panic overwhelmed him, but he tried to speak reasonably.

"I offer you gold, land, jewels. I cannot give you my nephew. He is his own man. He is not mine to give!"

"I did not ask you to *give* me the knight Gawain," she rebuked him. "If Gawain himself agrees to marry me, I will give you the answer. Those are my terms."

"Impossible!" he sputtered. "I could not bring him such a proposal."

"If you should change your mind, I will be here tomorrow," said she, and disappeared into the oak woods.

Shaken from the weird encounter, Arthur rode homeward at a slow pace.

"Save my own life at Gawain's expense? Never!" he thought. "Loathsome woman! I could not even speak of it to Gawain."

But the afternoon air was soft and sweet with birdsong, and the fateful meeting with Sir Gromer weighed on him heavily. He was torn by the terrible choice facing him.

Gawain rode out from the castle to meet the king. Seeing Arthur's pale, strained face, he exclaimed, "My lord! Are you ill? What has happened?"

"Nothing . . . nothing at all." But he could not keep silent long.

"The colossal impudence of the woman! A monster, that's what she is! That creature, daring to give me terms!"

"Calm yourself, uncle," Gawain said patiently. "What woman? Terms for what?"

Arthur sighed. "She knows the answer to the question. I didn't intend to tell you."

"Why not? Surely that's good news! What is the answer?"

"She will not tell me until her terms are met," said the king heavily. "But I assure you, I refuse to consider her proposal!"

Gawain smiled. "You talk in riddles yourself, uncle. Who is this woman who claims to know the answer? What is her proposal?"

Seeing Gawain's smiling, expectant face, Arthur at first could not speak. Then, with his eyes averted, the king told Gawain the whole story, leaving out no detail.

"The lady Ragnell is Sir Gromer's stepsister? Yes, I think she would know the right answer," Gawain said thoughtfully. "How fortunate that I will be able to save your life!"

"No! I will not let you sacrifice yourself!" Arthur cried.

"It is my choice and my decision," Gawain answered. "I will return with you tomorrow and agree to the marriage—on condition that the answer she supplies is the right one to save your life."

Early the following day, Gawain rode out with Arthur. But not even meeting the loathsome lady face to face could shake his resolve. Her proposal was accepted.

Gawain bowed courteously. "If on the morrow your answer saves the king's life, we will be wed."

On the fateful morning, Gawain watched the king stow a parchment in his saddlebag. "I'll try all these answers first," said Arthur.

They rode together for the first part of the journey. Then Arthur, unarmed as agreed, rode on alone to Inglewood to meet Sir Gromer.

The tall, powerful chieftain was waiting, his broadsword glinting in the sun.

Arthur read off one answer, then another, and another. Sir Gromer shook his head in satisfaction.

"No, you have not the right answer!" he said raising his sword high. "You've failed, and now—"

"Wait!" Arthur cried. "I have one more answer. What a woman desires above all else is the power of sovereignty—the right to exercise her own will."

With a loud oath the man dropped his sword. "You did not

find that answer by yourself!" he shouted. "My cursed stepsister, Ragnell, gave it to you. Bold, interfering hussy! I'll run her through with my sword . . . I'll lop off her head . . ." Turning, he plunged into the forest, a string of horrible curses echoing behind him.

Arthur rode back to where Gawain waited with the monstrous Ragnell. They returned to the castle in silence. Only the grotesque Lady Ragnell seemed in good spirits.

The news spread quickly throughout the castle. Gawain, the finest knight in the land, was to marry this monstrous creature! Some tittered and laughed at the spectacle; others said the lady Ragnell must possess very great lands and estates; but mostly there was stunned silence.

Arthur took his nephew aside nervously. "Must you go through with it at once? A postponement perhaps?"

Gawain looked at him steadily. "I gave my promise, my lord. The lady Ragnell's answer saved your life. Would you have me—"

"Your loyalty makes me ashamed! Of course you cannot break your word." And Arthur turned away.

The marriage took place in the abbey. Afterward, with Gawain and the lady Ragnell sitting at the high dais table beside the king and queen, the strange wedding feast began.

"She takes the space of two women on the chair," muttered the knight Gareth. "Poor Gawain!"

"I would not marry such a creature for all the land in Christendom!" answered his companion.

An uneasy silence settled on the hall. Only the monstrous Lady Ragnell displayed good spirits and good appetite. Throughout the long day and evening, Gawain remained pleasant and courteous. In no way did his manner toward his strange bride show other than kind attention.

The wedding feast drew to a close. Gawain and his bride were conducted to their chamber and were at last alone.

The lady Ragnell gazed at her husband thoughtfully.

"You have kept your promise well and faithfully," she observed.

Gawain inclined his head. "I could not do less, my lady."

"You've shown neither revulsion nor pity," she said. After a pause she went on, "Come now, we are wedded! I am waiting to be kissed."

Gawain went to her at once and kissed her. When he stepped back, there stood before him a slender young woman with gray eyes and a serene, smiling face.

His scalp tingled in shock. "What manner of sorcery is this?" he cried hoarsely.

"Do you prefer me in this form?" she smiled and turned slowly in a full circle.

But Gawain backed away warily. "I . . . yes . . . of course . . . but . . . I don't understand . . ." For this sudden evidence of sorcery, with its unknown powers, made him confused and uneasy.

"My stepbrother, Sir Gromer, had always hated me," said the lady Ragnell. "Unfortunately, through his mother, he has a knowledge of sorcery, and so he changed me into a monstrous creature. He said I must live in that shape until I could persuade the greatest knight in Britain to willingly choose me for his bride. He said it would be an impossible condition to meet!"

"Why did he hate you so cruelly?"

Her lips curled in amusement. "He thought me bold and unwomanly because I defied him. I refused his commands both for my property and my person.

Gawain said with admiration, "You won the 'impossible' condition he set, and now his evil spell is broken!"

"Only in part." Her clear gray eyes held his. "You have a choice, my dear Gawain, which way I will be. Would you have me in this, my own shape, at night and my former ugly shape by day? Or would you have me grotesque at night in our chamber, and my own shape in the castle by day? Think carefully before you choose."

Gawain was silent only a moment. He knelt before her and touched her hand.

"It is a choice I cannot make, my dear Ragnell. It concerns you. Whatever you choose to be—fair by day or fair by night—I will willingly abide by it."

Ragnell released a long, deep breath. The radiance in her face overwhelmed him.

"You have answered well, dearest Gawain, for your answer has broken Gromer's evil spell completely. The last condition he set has been met! For he said that if, after marriage to the greatest knight in Britain, my husband freely gave me the power of choice, the power to exercise my own free will, the wicked enchantment would be broken forever."

Thus, in wonder and in joy, began the marriage of Gawain and the lady Ragnell.

RESPONSE

1. Discuss the differences between the responses of Sir Gromer and Gawain to Lady Ragnell's demand for self-determination.

2. In what ways does contemporary society respond to an autonomous woman?

3. In what ways does contemporary society respond to an autonomous man?

4. Do you think that Gawain and Lady Ragnell love one another? Justify your answer.

EXTENSION

5. Lady Ragnell says, "my husband freely gave me the power of choice, the power to exercise my own free will. . . . " Does she really have the power of choice?

My Mother, My Rival

Mariah Burton Nelson

In what ways do you compete with others? Explain.

With whom do you compete most often? Explain.

What has competition taught you about yourself?

The first time my mother and I competed against each other she was 37; I was five. We swam one lap of our neighbor's pool. She won.

As a five-year-old I didn't realize—and I don't think my mother realized—that she was teaching me about love. We thought we were just fooling around.

Later we had diving competitions, which she also won, though I would argue, and she would concede, that I deserved higher marks for versatility. For my jackknife, I would *boing* into the air, desperately grab my toes, then splash down on all fours. For my back dive, I would reach my hands meekly overhead, then fall into the water as if I'd been shot. Mom had only one dive—the swan dive—but if you do only one dive you can learn to do it very well. She'd fly skyward, arch like a ship's proud figurehead, then streamline toward the water and quietly, tapered toes last, disappear.

Eventually I gave up diving—pointing my toes always seemed so unnatural—but I joined a swim team, and by the time I was 10, I could outswim Mom. ("Oh, I don't know about that," responds my mother now. "I think you were eleven.")

Mom was my fan, too, when I would race against Betty and Letty Landers, the indomitable twins at Cedarbrook Country Club in our mini-town of Blue Bell, Pennsylvania. Betty had skinny arms as sharp and swift as Osterizer blades; Letty had furious legs that started kicking mid-racing dive, like a windup bathtub toy. I didn't stand a chance.

But Mom would root for me anyway, yelling from the sidelines as if I could hear her underwater. She'd transport my friends and me to swimming meets all over the county (she liked to drive fast over the hilly, back-country roads so we'd fly up out of our seats and scream), and she even arranged practice time for me during family vacations to the New Jersey shore. It made me feel important to skip deep-sea fishing trips with my dad and siblings to work out at a pool.

Mom was also my teammate: the two of us ganged up on the Landers twins in the mother-daughter relay races at Cedarbrook's year-end championships. Mrs. Landers, a lounge lizard of sorts, had a great tan but no speed, so Mom and I were undefeated for six years until adolescence caught up with me and I left swimming for more important things, like basketball.

So when I think about competition I also remember the Landers twins, who would join me in the showers after the meets, the three of us giggling and whispering until all the hot water ran out. I think about Gordon, whom I later met on a basketball court; he would guard me by pushing on my waist with one hand and I still remember that push, and how much more honest it felt than my boyfriends' gropings. I remember six-foot-three-inch Heidi, my teammate, who would rebound the ball viciously, sharp elbows out; I hated her elbows but loved her audacity and her long strong hands, mirrors of my own. When I think about competition I realize that beginning with my fiercely, playfully competitive mother— who at 55 took up tennis and at 60 tried downhill skiing—athletes have taught me most of what I know about love.

Competition is about passion for perfection, and passion for other people who join in this impossible quest. What better way to get to know someone than to test your abilities together, to be daring and sweaty and exhausted together?

"If you compare yourself with others," a line in the inspirational prose poem "Desiderata" warns, "you may become vain and bitter, for always there will be greater and lesser persons than yourself." Yet I find that by comparing myself to other athletes, I become both self-confident and humble. Through competition, I have learned to acknowledge my failures and make allowances for the failures of others. Isn't that what intimacy is about?

But competition is not all fun and games. Like families, competitors can bring out the worst as well as the best in each other. Like romance, competition has many faces, some of them ugly. In addition to showing me my grace and graciousness, the mirror of sports has reflected back to me my jealousy, pettiness, and arrogance.

For instance: I have taken a friend to a tennis court, said, "Let's just hit a few," then fired the ball down her throat. I have, during a recreational, two-on-two volleyball game, refused to pass to my partner so that we could win.

Believing that "competitive" was a dirty word, I used to say, "I'm not competitive, I just happen to be the best." My teammate Heidi and I had a tearful yelling match one night after a basketball game, and I accused her of not passing me the ball. "How am I supposed to score more than 19 points if you won't even look in my direction?" I screamed. "Why are you so competitive with me?"

"Look who's being competitive!" she countered. "Since when is 19 points something to be ashamed of? Only when it's compared to my 29, right?"

Later I told friends, "I've realized that I am in fact very competitive."

"No!" they said sarcastically. "You?"

I guess I was the last to notice.

But despite such humiliations, Heidi and I are good friends, and because we have played basketball together, she knows me better than friends who only chat with me over lunch. I am never more naked than in the heat of competition. I never feel more vulnerable than after flubbing a catch in the ninth inning, or rolling a bowling ball into the gutter.

In sports, as in love, one can never pretend.

It is for this reason that some women avoid sports altogether; they choose not to unveil themselves in that way. In a society in which women's attractiveness is of utmost importance, why get muddy and sweaty and exhausted? Why risk anger, frustration, aggression, and other unseemly emotions? It is far safer to stay seated demurely in a café.

"I hate competition!" some friends have said to me. These are the women who were never taught how to throw or catch a ball, and I don't blame them. As an untrained musician, I know that if my childhood had been filled with music competitions, and I were chosen last for music teams and humiliated in front of other great musicians, I would resent both music and competition. Who enjoys doing things poorly?

A third reason many women have an ambivalent, if not downright hostile attitude toward sports—and why others embrace sports—is that team sports are an intense, physical activity. To play sports with women is to love women, to be passionate about women, to be intimate with women. How scary. Or, depending on your point of view, how thrilling.

So competition is about love, I noticed early, and, I noticed later, about fear. That's why I like to remember my childhood, when the love part was relatively pure, untainted by fear of failure, fear of looking like a fool, or fear of loving women. I feel blessed to have had a big brother who taught me how to throw, and a mother who never let me win. Even today, when I compete at water polo, bad-knee tennis, Nerf basketball, Ping-Pong, billiards—whatever I can persuade someone else to play with me—my favorite competitor is my mom. She is 63 now, I am 31, and when I visit her in Phoenix, we still race. "Give me a head start," she'll suggest, "or better yet, I'll do freestyle and you swim backstroke, just kicking, okay?" If she wins, she smacks her hand against the wall, jerks her head up, and yells, "Ha! Beat you!"

I complain that she must have cheated. She splashes me. I dunk her. We laugh a lot. And I think, yes, this must be love.

RESPONSE

1. Do you agree with Nelson that "Competition is about passion for perfection, and passion for other people who join in this impossible quest"? Explain.

2. Has Nelson proven to you that "In sports, as in love, one can never pretend"? Explain.

EXTENSION

3. Discuss the following question with members of your class: Do males compete differently from females?

4. a) Distinguish between an *opponent* and a *rival*.
   b) Compose an informal essay about a person who you consider to be a rival. Be sure to describe the nature of your rivalry.

E S S A Y

It's a Love Story

Kenneth Gergen and Mary Gergen

> What features of the traditional love story do you want in your own romantic relationships?
>
> What aspects of the traditional love story will you change in your own romantic relationships? Why?

When a man and a woman privately whisper sweet nothings, a whole society is feeding them their lines. How they behave and even how they feel depend, in part, on a host of myths they learned from their society—modified by each partner's experiences. As a relationship grows, a new myth is born: the narrative the partners develop together about themselves as a couple—who they are, what they owe one another, where they've been and where they're headed.

In very stable, traditional cultures most of the narrative has been set in stone by the society. But in our own culture, recent changes have drastically altered our traditional social myths, making the rules of the game inconsistent and placing more pressure on us to shape and make sense of our relationships. Still, our very private lives reflect our times and our setting.

During the late 1800s and the first half of the 1900s the traditional "love story," in which two young people see themselves as "in love" and start to build an enduring relationship, became a popular social convention, at least in the United States. The love story as we know it was probably invented by women during the industrial revolution to control the increasing independence of men from the family. Something had to replace the "rights and duties" that were once the traditional "glue" of relationships. It was greatly to women's advantage if sexual desire could be interpreted as "love" and a man's desires for her could result in lasting commitment and economic security. By romanticizing lust as love and attaching conditions to its expression, women could gain some control over men. A man who was attracted to a woman and wanted a sexual relationship would be required to enter into a tale about the two of them that included long-term commitments to caring for her and her offspring.

Because women benefited from this arrangement, they became the keepers of the romantic tale and specialists in the ways of emotion talk. Men who wanted women had to learn to participate in these narratives and say the right words. In effect, they had to succumb to the power of the "love story."

But in the past 30 years some dramatic changes in women's social condition have changed our narratives of relationship and our lifestyles. These changes began to occur during World War II, when women were called upon to do what society had once seen as exclusively "men's work." This lesson in independence was not lost on subsequent generations of women.

Yet the narrative of the postwar American society was a return to the traditional sex roles, built on the foundation of breadwinning man and his homemaking wife, who cared for the children. This happy family story, which did not recognize the growing involvement of women in the labor force, served the nation through the Eisenhower days.

But by the early 1960s, prosperity, a huge labor force of women and the Pill all converged. Women went to school, got jobs and worked full time after they were married, even when they had children. They independently controlled their own pregnancies, and they began to think about sex as something personally gratifying, not exclusively as an expression of love. As women began to live without depending on a man, the place that had a man at the center of a woman's emotional life began to disintegrate.

By the '70s, dual-career marriage became commonplace. Couples delayed getting married, and pregnancies became planned. Children were likely to be seen as the couple's mutual "property," with both partners having equal responsibilities for caretaking. Relationships were not necessarily forever, and divorce was written into the scripts; the couple became partners for as long as the relationship was good. Men and women had adopted a language of relationships that allowed each greater freedom and financial independence. If women were the keepers of the romantic flame, they had turned the gas on low.

As one might have predicted when women substituted career stories for love stories, emotional expressions and related behavioral patterns became confused. By 1974, as George Orwell had anticipated, "love," at least as it had been understood, was almost dead. Women were discovering that having a job could be as rewarding and financially secure as having a man, or more so. The singles scene was in full swing, and sexual narratives flourished with barely a word about relationships or love. "The one night stand" story meant never having to say "hello."

It was a confusing transitional period for young people. The new themes of looking out for number one, taking advantage of every situation and achieving one's full potential clashed with the more traditional notions of sharing one's good times and bad, having children, building a family and growing old together. In effect, during the past 30 years, the "heart" of the relational narrative was bypassed. Emotions lost their power as rhetorical motives, and personal narratives became more central. Like Frank Sinatra, people increasingly took pride in the claim: "I did it my way."

But our story is not over. It looks as if narratives of relationship are being revived and "love" is on the rebound. Two major factors may underlie this shift. First, many women, even those "in love" with their careers, find themselves wanting to have children, and most women want them to be raised within a family circle. For some period of their lives, at least, women want to find someone with whom they can share this vision of family life. Like the women who long ago looked for a man to protect them during their times of childbearing, today's women also want that bond and are looking for someone who will complement a "love story with baby."

The second factor, one possibly of even greater significance, is the AIDS epidemic. Fear of AIDS is making casual sex passé. Sex is becoming reconnected with emotional commitments as a new chastity settles on the land. Between wanting babies and "safe" sexual relations, young adults are resuscitating "love" talk. True, it's tempered by pragmatic considerations, but love is no longer a four-letter word, and commitment is once again voluntary—even by men. It will be interesting to see whether new relationship narratives will be formed on the basis of "love," in the traditional sense, or if new emotional terms, new types of agreements or new narratives will emerge to define a couple. Whatever the future holds, it's clear that in understanding relationships, what counts is not the "reality of things" but how symbolic events woven into the stories of life create and control even our most private lives.

RESPONSE

1. Do you agree with the following statement: "How they [a man and a woman] behave and even how they feel depend, in part, on a host of myths they learned from their society"?

2. According to the authors, what were the bases of the traditional love story before the twentieth century?

3. Discuss some possibilities for new types of agreements and new narratives which might form the bases of new relationships.

EXTENSION

4. Examine the nature of a marital relationship as depicted in a television series or film. Present your findings to the class.

5. Examine the nature of a family relationship as depicted in a television series or film. Present your findings to the class.

6. Write a journal entry, commenting on the strengths and weaknesses of the relationships you examined in questions 4 and 5.

The
Earth
And Us

Science's Method Misunderstood

Fernand Seguin

> What do you understand to be the scientific method?
>
> What do you think is the purpose of science? Explain.

The growing rift between the scientific community and the general public has been deplored time and time again. The problem isn't a loss of prestige by scientists (they still enjoy a great deal of credibility with the public) nor is it any longer a question of science's difficult technical vocabulary. Thanks to the media, scientific terms are now made clear to the public, and many have become a part of everyday language despite the fact that their precise connotations are not always understood.

The reasons for this widening gap between the two cultures, between lawyer and doctor, union organizer and neurologist, politician and epidemiologist, decision maker and experimental researcher, are not found in the public's awareness of scientific concepts and issues, but in the lack of appreciation of how the scientific method itself works; scientific logic is still largely misunderstood by non-scientists. This gap, with all its harmful consequences in the social, political, economic and even military fields, will not be closed by introducing scientific and technical programs into the educational system unless these studies include fundamental explanations of the scientific method.

Consider, for example, the concept of comparative experimentation; this approach, routinely employed in checking the effectiveness of new drugs by medical researchers, utilizes two groups of subjects (they can be animal or human) that exhibit the same general characteristics and suffer from the same illness; one group receives the drug and the second or control group is given a harmless substance (of identical appearance) that contains no active ingredients; this latter "drug" is called a placebo. The drug's effectiveness is evaluated by comparing the results obtained in the experimental group with those of the control group. One might consider it to be cruel to submit a group of sick people to such clinical research, in which half the subjects will be given a nonexistent drug and whose health will presumably continue to deteriorate. But, it is the best method of evaluating the effectiveness of a pharmaceutical product and a process that very few people outside of science appreciate. Thus, there is no such thing as absolute certainty in the results of experimental research; if the public were more aware of this, there would not be the current, creeping lack of faith in science.

There is also the problem of misuse of the methods of science, particularly by advertisers on television. For example, a product against the flu is shown and the announcer claims that it helps to relieve the symptoms. He does not say that the product is a cure, because Canadian advertising regulations forbid this. But the advertiser plays on the fact that the unwary viewer, who is also bombarded by commercials that are as enthusiastic as they are ambiguous, does not always make the distinction between a product that cures and one that merely "helps to relieve."

In this television example, the scientific approach would involve comparing the results of two identical groups of flu sufferers; one group would receive the syrup and the other a placebo solution. Advertising would become, without a doubt, less vociferous.

Another abuse of the scientific method is in the application of statistics in cases where they have no value. People fail to realize that statistics only apply to events that are sufficiently numerous to allow probability calculations to be made. Thus, life insurance companies, knowing the mortality tables for the population as a whole, can evaluate an individual's chances of still being alive at seventy and thus calculate the cost of insurance premiums with a minimal risk of error.

But when the weatherman, either on radio or on television, states with calm assurance that the risk of precipitation for tomorrow is 30 per cent, this prediction has absolutely no value. What he is trying to say is that, if the current meteorological conditions were identical to those of a hundred previous cases (which would be impossible to evaluate exactly), and if the development of these conditions were also identical to those already compiled, there would be snow or rain tomorrow in 30 per cent of the cases.

The problem is that there is only one tomorrow, so that the statistical calculation does not apply. There is no quantitative statistical method for this type of event. The most that the meteorologist can say is that it probably will snow or rain. This is the kind of prediction that can be made without having a university degree and without using computers, by anyone who lives close to Nature and who observes the winds and the clouds. The concept of "30 per cent chance" is a gross misuse of scientific logic.

The Science Council of Canada is right in recommending an increase in the quality and quantity of science taught in Canada at all levels. What ought to be added, however, is that this teaching should not be confused with the mere transmission of scientific knowledge. The important thing is to appreciate the scientific method itself, the manner of its mechanism; scientists first observe, then formulate hypotheses or explanations of how things might work; next they test these ideas through experiments and finally draw conclusions from the experimental results; the process is nothing more than the application of simple common sense.

In an age when it will soon be impossible to buy a sheet of plywood without a degree, it is useful to point out that learning the scientific method is within everybody's grasp.

RESPONSE

1. In your own words, explain the scientific method as understood by Seguin.

2. Select and explain two examples from the essay which show the misuse of the scientific method.

3. Do you agree that the scientific method is nothing more than the application of simple common sense? Explain.

EXTENSION

4. Examine the ways in which science and scientists are portrayed in contemporary movies and television. Using a specific example, present your observations to the class.

5. Write a journal entry about the degree to which you feel comfortable or uncomfortable with the role of contemporary science and technology.

6. Debate the following statement: The scientific community is worthy of trust.

7. Invite a science teacher to your class to respond to Seguin's essay.

How Flowers Changed the World

Loren Eiseley

> What are the purposes of flowers?
>
> What is your favourite flower? Why?

If it had been possible to observe the earth from the far side of the solar system over the long course of geological epochs, the watchers might have been able to discern a subtle change in the light emanating from our planet. That world of long ago would, like the red deserts of Mars, have reflected light from vast drifts of stone and gravel, the sands of wandering wastes, the blackness of naked basalt, the yellow dust of endlessly moving storms. Only the ceaseless marching of the clouds and the intermittent flashes from the restless surface of the sea would have told a different story, but still essentially a barren one. Then, as the millennia rolled away and age followed age, a new and greener light would, by degrees, have come to twinkle across those endless miles.

This is the only difference those far watchers, by the use of subtle instruments, might have perceived in the whole history of the planet Earth. Yet that slowly growing green twinkle would have contained the epic march of life from the tidal oozes upward across the raw and unclothed continents. Out of the vast chemical bath of the sea—not from the deeps, but from the element-rich, light-exposed platforms of the continental shelves—wandering fingers of green had crept upward along the meanderings of river systems and fringed the gravels of forgotten lakes.

In those first ages plants clung of necessity to swamps and watercourses. Their reproductive processes demanded direct access to water. Beyond the primitive ferns and mosses that enclosed the borders of swamps and streams the rocks still lay vast and bare, the winds still swirled the dust of a naked planet. The grass cover that holds our world secure in place was still millions of years in the future. The green marchers had gained a soggy foothold upon the land, but that was all. They did not reproduce by seeds but by microscopic swimming sperm that had to wriggle their way through water to fertilize the female cell. Such plants in their higher forms had clever adaptations for the use of rain water in their sexual phases and survived with increasing success in a wet land environment. They now seem part of man's normal environment. The truth is, however, that there is nothing very "normal" about nature. Once upon a time there were no flowers at all.

A little while ago—about one hundred million years, as the geologist estimates time in the history of our four-billion-year-old planet—flowers were not to be found anywhere on the five continents. Wherever one might have looked, from the poles to the equator, one would have seen only the cold dark monotonous green of a world whose plant life possessed no other color.

Somewhere, just a short time before the close of the Age of Reptiles, there occurred a soundless, violent explosion. It lasted millions of years, but it was an explosion, nevertheless. It marked the emergence of the angiosperms—the flowering plants. Even the great evolutionist Charles Darwin called them "an abominable mystery," because they appeared so suddenly and spread so fast.

Flowers changed the face of the planet. Without them, the world we know—even man himself—would never have existed. Francis Thompson, the English poet, once wrote that one could not pluck a flower without troubling a star. Intuitively he had sensed like a naturalist the enormous interlinked complexity of life. Today we know that the appearance of the flowers contained also the equally mystifying emergence of man.

If we were to go back into the Age of Reptiles, its drowned swamps and birdless forests would reveal to us a warmer but, on the whole, a sleepier world than that of today. Here and there, it is true, the serpent heads of bottom-feeding dinosaurs might be upreared in suspicion of their huge flesh-eating compatriots. Tyrannosaurs, enormous bipedal caricatures of men, would stalk mindlessly across the sites of future cities and go their slow way down into the dark of geologic time.

In all that world of living things nothing saw save with the intense concentration of the hunt, nothing moved except with the grave sleepwalking intentness of the instinct-driven brain. Judged by modern standards, it was a world in slow motion, a cold-blooded world whose occupants were most active at noonday but torpid on chill nights, their brains damped by a slower metabolism than any known to even the most primitive of warm-blooded animals today.

A high metabolic rate and the maintenance of a constant body temperature are supreme achievements in the evolution of life. They enable an animal to escape, within broad limits, from the overheating or the chilling of its immediate surroundings, and at the same time to maintain a peak mental efficiency. Creatures without a high metabolic rate are slaves to weather. Insects in the first frosts of autumn all run down like little clocks. Yet if you pick one up and breathe warmly upon it, it will begin to move about once more.

In a sheltered spot such creatures may sleep away the winter, but they are hopelessly immobilized. Though a few warm-blooded mammals, such as the woodchuck of our day, have evolved a way of reducing their metabolic rate in order to undergo winter hibernation, it is a survival mechanism with drawbacks, for it leaves the animal helplessly exposed if enemies discover him during his period of suspended animation. Thus bear or woodchuck, big animal or small, must seek, in this time of descending sleep, a safe refuge in some hidden den or burrow. Hibernation is, therefore, primarily a winter refuge of small, easily concealed animals rather than of large ones.

A high metabolic rate, however, means a heavy intake of energy in order to sustain body warmth and efficiency. It is for this reason that even some of these later warm-blooded mammals existing in our day have learned to descend into a slower, unconscious rate of living during the winter months when food may be difficult to obtain. On a slightly higher plane they are following the procedure of the cold-blooded frog sleeping in the mud at the bottom of a frozen pond.

The agile brain of the warm-blooded birds and mammals demands a high oxygen consumption and food in concentrated forms, or the creatures cannot long sustain themselves. It was the rise of the flowering plants that provided that energy and changed the nature of the living world. Their appearance parallels in a quite surprising manner the rise of the birds and mammals.

Slowly, toward the dawn of the Age of Reptiles, something over two hundred and fifty million years ago, the little naked sperm cells wriggling their way through dew and raindrops had given way to a kind of pollen carried by the wind. Our present-day pine forests represent plants of a pollen-disseminating variety. Once fertilization was no longer dependent on exterior water, the march over drier regions could be extended. Instead of spores, simple primitive seeds carrying some nourishment for the young plant had developed, but true flowers were still scores of millions of years away. After a long period of hesitant evolutionary groping, they exploded upon the world with truly revolutionary violence.

The event occurred in Cretaceous times in the close of the Age of Reptiles. Before the coming of the flowering plants our own ancestral stock, the warm-blooded mammals, consisted of a few mousy little creatures hidden in trees and underbrush. A few lizard-like birds with carnivorous teeth flapped awkwardly on ill-aimed flights among archaic shrubbery. None of these insignificant creatures gave evidence of any remarkable talents. The mammals in particular had been around for some millions of years but had remained well lost in the shadow of the mighty reptiles. Truth to tell, man was still, like the genie in the bottle, encased in the body of a creature about the size of a rat.

As for the birds, their reptilian cousins the Pterodactyls flew farther and better. There was just one thing about the birds that paralleled the physiology of the mammals. They, too, had evolved warm blood and its accompanying temperature control. Nevertheless, if one had been seen stripped of his feathers, he would still have seemed a slightly uncanny and unsightly lizard.

Neither the birds nor the mammals, however, were quite what they seemed. They were waiting for the Age of Flowers. They were waiting for what flowers, and with them the true encased seed, would bring. Fish-eating, gigantic, leather-winged reptiles, twenty-eight feet from wing tip to wing tip, hovered over the coasts that one day would be swarming with gulls.

Inland the monotonous green of the pine and spruce forests with their primitive wooden cone flowers stretched everywhere. No grass hindered the fall of the naked seeds to earth. Great sequoias towered to the skies. The world of that time has a certain appeal but it is a giant's world, a world moving slowly like the reptiles who stalked magnificently among the boles of its trees.

The trees themselves are ancient, slow-growing, and immense, like the redwood groves that have survived to our day on the California coast. All is stiff, formal, upright and green, monotonously green. There is no grass as yet; there are no wide plains rolling in the sun, no tiny daisies dotting the meadows underfoot. There is little versatility about this scene; it is, in truth, a giant's world.

A few nights ago it was brought home vividly to me that the world has changed since that far epoch. I was awakened out of sleep by an unknown sound in my living room. Not a small sound—not a creaking timber or a mouse's scurry—but a sharp, rending explosion as though an unwary foot had been put down upon a wine glass. I had come instantly out of sleep and lay tense, unbreathing. I listened for another step. There was none.

Unable to stand the suspense any longer, I turned on the light and passed from room to room glancing uneasily behind chairs and into closets. Nothing seemed disturbed, and I stood puzzled in the center of the living room floor. Then a small button-shaped object upon the rug caught my eye. It was hard and polished and glistening. Scattered over the length of the room were several more, shining up at me like wary little eyes. A pine cone that had been lying in a dish had been blown the length of the coffee table. The dish itself could hardly have been the source of the explosion. Beside it I found two ribbonlike strips of a velvety-green. I tried to place the two strips together to make a pod. They twisted resolutely away from each other and would no longer fit.

I relaxed in a chair, then, for I had reached a solution of the midnight disturbance. The twisted strips were wistaria pods that I had brought in a day or two previously and placed in the dish. They had chosen midnight to explode and distribute their multiplying fund of life down the length of the room. A plant, a fixed, rooted thing, immobilized in a single spot, had devised a way of propelling its offspring across open space. Immediately there passed before my eyes the million airy troopers of the milkweed pod and the clutching hooks of the sandburs. Seeds on the coyote's tail, seeds on the hunter's coat, thistledown mounting on the winds—all were somehow triumphing over life's limitations. Yet the ability to do this had not been with them at the beginning. It was the product of endless effort and experiment.

The seeds on my carpet were not going to lie stiffly where they had dropped like their antiquated cousins, the naked seeds on the pine-cone scales. They were travelers. Struck by the thought, I went out next day and collected several other varieties. I line them up now in a row on my desk—so many little capsules of life, winged, hooked or spiked. Every one is an angiosperm, a product of the true flowering plants. Contained in these little boxes is the secret of that far-off Cretaceous explosion of a hundred million years ago that changed the face of the planet. And somewhere in here, I think, as I poke seriously at one particularly resistant seedcase of a wild grass, was once man himself.

When the first simple flower bloomed on some raw upland late in the Dinosaur Age, it was wind-pollinated, just like its early pine-cone relatives. It was a very inconspicuous flower because it had not yet evolved the idea of using the surer attraction of birds and insects to achieve the transportation of pollen. It sowed its own pollen and received the pollen of other flowers by the simple vagaries of the wind. Many plants in regions where insect life is scant still follow this principle today. Nevertheless, the true flower—and the seed that it produced—was a profound innovation in the world of life.

In a way, this event parallels, in the plant world, what happened among animals. Consider the relative chance for survival of the exteriorly deposited egg of a fish in contrast with the fertilized egg of a mammal, carefully retained for months in the mother's body until the young animal (or human being) is developed to a point where it may survive. The biological wastage is less—and so it is with the flowering plants. The primitive spore, a single cell fertilized in the beginning by a swimming sperm, did not promote rapid distribution, and the young plant, moreover, had to struggle up from nothing. No one had left it any food except what it could get by its own unaided efforts.

By contrast, the true flowering plants (angiosperm itself means "encased seed") grew a seed in the heart of a flower, a seed whose development was initiated by a fertilizing pollen grain independent of outside moisture. But the seed, unlike the developing spore, is already a fully equipped *embryonic plant* packed in a little enclosed box stuffed full of nutritious food. Moreover, by featherdown attachments, as in dandelion or milkweed seed, it can be wafted upward on gusts and ride the wind for miles; or with hooks it can cling to a bear's or a rabbit's hide; or like some of the berries, it can be covered with a juicy, attractive fruit to lure birds, pass undigested through their intestinal tracts, and be voided miles away.

The ramifications of this biological invention were endless. Plants traveled as they had never traveled before. They got into strange environments heretofore never entered by the old spore plants or stiff pine-cone-seed plants. The well-fed, carefully cherished little embryos raised their heads everywhere. Many of the older plants with more primitive reproductive mechanisms began to fade away under this unequal contest. They contracted their range into secluded environments. Some, like the giant redwoods, lingered on as relics; many vanished entirely.

The world of the giants was a dying world. These fantastic little seeds skipping and hopping and flying about the woods and valleys brought with them an amazing adaptability. If our whole lives had not been spent in the midst of it, it would astound us. The old, stiff, sky-reaching wooden world had changed into something that glowed here and there with strange colors, put out queer, unheard-of fruits and little intricately carved seed cases, and, most important of all, produced concentrated foods in a way that the land had never seen before, or dreamed of back in the fish-eating, leaf-crunching days of the dinosaurs.

That food came from three sources, all produced by the reproductive system of the flowering plants. There were the tantalizing nectars and pollens intended to draw insects for pollenizing purposes, and which are responsible also for that wonderful jeweled creation, the hummingbird. There were the juicy and enticing fruits to attract larger animals, and in which tough-coated seeds were concealed, as in the tomato, for example. Then, as if this were not enough, there was the food in the actual seed itself, the food intended to nourish the embryo. All over the world, like hot corn in a popper, these incredible elaborations of the flowering plants kept exploding. In a movement that was almost instantaneous, geologically speaking, the angiosperms had taken over the world. Grass was beginning to cover the bare earth until, today, there are over six thousand species. All kinds of vines and bushes squirmed and writhed under new trees with flying seeds.

The explosion was having its effect on animal life also. Specialized groups of insects were arising to feed on the new sources of food and, incidentally and unknowingly, to pollinate the plant. The flowers bloomed and bloomed in ever larger and more spectacular varieties. Some were pale unearthly night flowers intended to lure moths in the evening twilight, some among the orchids even took the shape of female spiders in order to attract wandering males, some flamed redly in the light of noon or twinkled modestly in the meadow grasses. Intricate mechanisms splashed pollen on the breasts of hummingbirds or stamped it on the bellies of black, grumbling bees droning assiduously from blossom to blossom. Honey ran, insects multiplied, and even the descendants of that toothed and ancient lizard-bird had become strangely altered. Equipped with prodding beaks instead of biting teeth they pecked the seeds and gobbled the insects that were really converted nectar.

Across the planet grasslands were now spreading. A slow continental upthrust which had been a part of the early Age of Flowers had cooled the world's climates. The stalking reptiles and the leather-winged black imps of the seashore cliffs had vanished. Only birds roamed the air now, hot-blooded and high-speed metabolic machines.

The mammals, too, had survived and were venturing into new domains, staring about perhaps a bit bewildered at their sudden eminence now that the thunder lizards were gone. Many of them, beginning as small browsers upon leaves in the forest, began to venture out upon this new sunlit world of the grass. Grass has a high silica content and demands a new type of very tough and resistant tooth enamel, but the seeds taken incidentally in the cropping of the grass are highly nutritious. A new world had opened out for the warm-blooded mammals. Great herbivores like the mammoths, horses, and bisons appeared. Skulking about them had arisen savage flesh-feeding carnivores like the now extinct dire wolves and the saber-toothed tiger.

Flesh eaters though these creatures were, they were being sustained on nutritious grasses one step removed. Their fierce energy was being maintained on a high, effective level, through hot days and frosty nights, by the concentrated energy of the angiosperms. That energy, thirty per cent or more of the weight of the entire plant among some of the cereal grasses, was being accumulated and concentrated in the rich proteins and fats of the enormous game herds of the grasslands.

On the edge of the forest, a strange, old-fashioned animal still hesitated. His body was the body of a tree dweller, and though tough and knotty by human standards, he was, in terms of that world into which he gazed, a weakling. His teeth, though strong for chewing on the tough fruits of the forest, or for crunching an occasional unwary bird caught with his prehensile hands, were not the tearing sabers of the great cats. He had a passion for lifting himself up to see about, in his restless, roving curiosity. He would run, a little stiffly and uncertainly perhaps, on his hind legs, but only in those rare moments when he ventured out upon the ground. All this was the legacy of his climbing days; he had a hand with flexible fingers and no fine specialized hoofs upon which to gallop like the wind.

If he had any idea of competing in that new world, he had better forget it; teeth or hooves, he was much too late for either. He was a ne'er-do-well, an in-betweener. Nature had not done well by him. It was as if she had hesitated and never quite made up her mind. Perhaps as a consequence he had a malicious gleam in his eye, the gleam of an outcast who has been left nothing and knows he is going to have to take what he gets. One day a little band of these odd apes—for apes they were—shambled out upon the grass; the human story had begun.

Apes were to become men, in the inscrutable wisdom of nature, because flowers had produced seeds and fruits in such tremendous quantities that a new and totally different store of energy had become available in concentrated form. Impressive as the slow-moving, dim-brained dinosaurs had been, it is doubtful if their age had supported anything like the diversity of life that now rioted across the planet or flashed in and out among the trees. Down on the grass by a streamside, one of those apes with inquisitive fingers turned over a stone and hefted it vaguely. The group clucked together in a throaty tongue and moved off through the tall grass foraging for seeds and insects. The one still held, sniffed, and hefted the stone he had found. He liked the feel of it in his fingers. The attack on the animal world was about to begin.

If one could run the story of that first human group like a speeded-up motion picture through a million years of time, one might see the stone in the hand change to the flint ax and the torch. All that swarming grassland world with its giant bison and trumpeting mammoths would go down in ruin to feed the insatiable and growing numbers of a carnivore who, like the great cats before him, was taking his energy indirectly from the grass. Later he found fire and it altered the tough meats and drained their energy even faster into a stomach ill adapted for the ferocious turn man's habits had taken.

His limbs grew longer, he strode more purposefully over the grass. The stolen energy that would take man across the continents would fail him at last. The great Ice Age herds were destined to vanish. When they did so, another hand like the hand that grasped the stone by the river long ago would pluck a handful of grass seed and hold it contemplatively.

In that moment, the golden towers of man, his swarming

millions, his turning wheels, the vast learning of his packed libraries, would glimmer dimly there in the ancestor of wheat, a few seeds held in a muddy hand. Without the gift of flowers and the infinite diversity of their fruits, man and bird, if they had continued to exist at all, would be today unrecognizable. Archaeopteryx, the lizard-bird, might still be snapping at beetles on a sequoia limb; man might still be a nocturnal insectivore gnawing a roach in the dark. The weight of a petal has changed the face of the world and made it ours.

RESPONSE

1. What do you think the author means when he writes "there is nothing very 'normal' about nature"?

2. Trace the history of the relationship between flowers and mammals.

3. What does Eiseley mean when he says that "Apes were to become men . . . because flowers had produced seeds and fruits"? Has he convinced you? Why or why not?

EXTENSION

4. Read "A Sound of Thunder" (p. 189). Discuss the story in a small group and compare its theme to the premise of Eiseley's essay.

A Sound of Thunder

Ray Bradbury

> What personal daily choices do you make which could have long-term effects upon the environment of the planet?

The sign on the wall seemed to quaver under a film of sliding warm water. Eckels felt his eyelids blink over his stare, and the sign burned in this momentary darkness:

TIME SAFARI, INC.
SAFARIS TO ANY YEAR IN THE PAST.
YOU NAME THE ANIMAL.
WE TAKE YOU THERE.
YOU SHOOT IT.

A warm phlegm gathered in Eckels' throat; he swallowed and pushed it down. The muscles around his mouth formed a smile as he put his hand slowly out upon the air, and in that hand waved a check for ten thousand dollars to the man behind the desk.

"Does this safari guarantee I come back alive?"

"We guarantee nothing," said the official, "except the dinosaurs." He turned. "This is Mr. Travis, your Safari Guide in the Past. He'll tell you what and where to shoot. If he says no shooting, no shooting. If you disobey instructions, there's a stiff penalty of another ten thousand dollars, plus possible government action, on your return."

Eckels glanced across the vast office at a mass and tangle, a snaking and humming of wires and steel boxes, at an aurora that flickered now orange, now silver, now blue. There was a sound like a gigantic bonfire burning all of Time, all the years and all the parchment calendars, all the hours piled high and set aflame.

A touch of the hand and this burning would, on the instant,

A Sound of Thunder **189**

beautifully reverse itself. Eckels remembered the wording in the advertisements to the letter. Out of chars and ashes, out of dust and coals, like golden salamanders, the old years, the green years, might leap; roses sweeten the air, white hair turn Irish-black, wrinkles vanish; all, everything fly back to seed, flee death, rush down to their beginnings, suns rise in western skies and set in glorious easts, moons eat themselves opposite to the custom, all and everything cupping one in another like Chinese boxes, rabbits into hats, all and everything returning to the fresh death, the seed death, the green death, to the time before the beginning. A touch of a hand might do it, the merest touch of a hand.

"Hell and damn," Eckels breathed, the light of the Machine on his thin face. "A real Time Machine." He shook his head. "Makes you think. If the election had gone badly yesterday, I might be here now running away from the results. Thank God Keith won. He'll make a fine President of the United States."

"Yes," said the man behind the desk. "We're lucky. If Deutscher had gotten in, we'd have the worst kind of dictatorship. There's an anti-everything man for you, a militarist, anti-Christ, anti-human, anti-intellectual. People called us up, you know, joking but not joking. Said if Deutscher became President they wanted to go live in 1492. Of course it's not our business to conduct Escapes, but to form Safaris. Anyway, Keith's President now. All you got to worry about is—"

"Shooting my dinosaur," Eckels finished it for him.

"A *Tyrannosaurus rex*. The Thunder Lizard, the damnedest monster in history. Sign this release. Anything happens to you, we're not responsible. Those dinosaurs are hungry."

Eckels flushed angrily. "Trying to scare me!"

"Frankly, yes. We don't want anyone going who'll panic at the first shot. Six Safari leaders were killed last year, and a dozen hunters. We're here to give you the damnedest thrill a *real* hunter ever asked for. Traveling you back sixty million years to bag the biggest damned game in all Time. Your personal check's still there. Tear it up."

Mr. Eckels looked at the check for a long time. His fingers twitched.

"Good luck," said the man behind the desk. "Mr. Travis, he's all yours."

They moved silently across the room, taking their guns with them, toward the Machine, toward the silver metal and the roaring light.

First a day and then a night and then a day and then a night, then it was day-night-day-night-day. A week, a month, a year, a decade! A.D. 2055. A.D. 2019. 1999! 1957! Gone! The Machine roared.

They put on their oxygen helmets and tested the intercoms.

Eckels swayed on the padded seat, his face pale, his jaw stiff. He felt the trembling in his arms and he looked down and found his hands tight on the new rifle. There were four other men in the Machine. Travis, the Safari Leader, his assistant, Lesperance, and two other hunters, Billings and Kramer. They sat looking at each other, and the years blazed around them.

"Can these guns get a dinosaur cold?" Eckels felt his mouth saying.

"If you hit them right," said Travis on the helmet radio. "Some dinosaurs have two brains, one in the head, another far down the spinal column. We stay away from those. That's stretching luck. Put your first two shots into the eyes, if you can, blind them, and go back into the brain."

The Machine howled. Time was a film run backward. Suns fled and ten million moons fled after them. "Good God," said Eckels. "Every hunter that ever lived would envy us today. This makes Africa seem like Illinois."

The Machine slowed; its scream fell to a murmur. The Machine stopped.

The sun stopped in the sky.

The fog that had enveloped the Machine blew away and they were in an old time, a very old time indeed, three hunters and two Safari Heads with their blue metal guns across their knees.

"Christ isn't born yet," said Travis. "Moses has not gone to the mountain to talk with God. The Pyramids are still in the earth, waiting to be cut out and put up. *Remember* that. Alexander, Caesar, Napoleon, Hitler—none of them exists."

The men nodded.

"That"—Mr. Travis pointed—"is the jungle of sixty million two thousand and fifty-five years before President Keith."

He indicated a metal path that struck off into green wilderness, over steaming swamp, among giant ferns and palms.

"And that," he said, "is the Path, laid by Time Safari for your use. It floats six inches above the earth. Doesn't touch so much as one grass blade, flower, or tree. It's an anti-gravity metal. Its purpose is to keep you from touching this world of the past in any way. Stay on the Path. Don't go off it. I repeat. *Don't go off.* For *any* reason! If you fall off, there's a penalty. And don't shoot any animal we don't okay."

"Why?" asked Eckels.

They sat in the ancient wilderness. Far birds' cries blew on a wind, and the smell of tar and an old salt sea, moist grasses, and flowers the color of blood.

"We don't want to change the Future. We don't belong here in the Past. The government doesn't *like* us here. We have to pay big graft to keep our franchise. A Time Machine is damn finicky business. Not knowing it, we might kill an important animal, a small bird, a roach, a flower even, thus destroying an important link in a growing species."

"That's not clear," said Eckels.

"All right," Travis continued, "say we accidentally kill one mouse here. That means all the future families of this one particular mouse are destroyed, right?"

"Right."

"And all the families of the families of the families of that one mouse! With a stamp of your foot, you annihilate first one, then a dozen, then a thousand, a million, a *billion* possible mice!"

"So they're dead," said Eckels. "So what?"

"So what?" Travis snorted quietly. "Well, what about the foxes that'll need those mice to survive? For want of ten mice, a fox dies. For want of ten foxes, a lion starves. For want of a lion, all manner of insects, vultures, infinite billions of life forms are thrown into chaos and destruction. Eventually it all boils down to this: fifty-nine million years later, a cave man, one of a dozen on the *entire world*, goes hunting wild boar or saber-tooth tiger for food. But you, friend, have *stepped* on all the tigers in that region. By stepping on *one* single mouse. So the cave man starves. And the cave man, please note, is not just *any* expendable man, no! He is an *entire future nation*. From his loins would have sprung ten sons. From *their* loins one hundred sons, and thus onward to a civilization. Destroy this one man, and you destroy a race, a people, an entire history of life. It is comparable to slaying some of Adam's grandchildren. The stomp of your foot, on one mouse, could start an earthquake, the effects of which could shake our earth and destinies down through Time, to their very foundations. With the death of that one cave man, a billion others yet unborn are throttled in the womb. Perhaps Rome never rises on its seven hills. Perhaps Europe is forever a dark forest, and only Asia waxes healthy and teeming. Step on a mouse and you crush the Pyramids. Step on a mouse and you leave your print, like a Grand Canyon, across Eternity. Queen

Elizabeth might never be born, Washington might not cross the Delaware, there might never be a United States at all. So be careful. Stay on the Path. *Never* step off!"

"I see," said Eckels. "Then it wouldn't pay for us even to touch the *grass*?"

"Correct. Crushing certain plants could add up infinitesimally. A little error here would multiply in sixty million years, all out of proportion. Of course maybe our theory is wrong. Maybe Time *can't* be changed by us. Or maybe it can be changed only in little subtle ways. A dead mouse here makes an insect imbalance there, a population disproportion later, a bad harvest further on, a depression, mass starvation, and, finally, a change in *social* temperament in far-flung countries. Something much more subtle, like that. Perhaps only a soft breath, a whisper, a hair, pollen on the air, such a slight, slight change that unless you looked close you wouldn't see it. Who knows? Who really can say he knows? We don't know. We're guessing. But until we do know for certain whether our messing around in Time *can* make a big roar or a little rustle in history, we're being damned careful. This Machine, this Path, your clothing and bodies, were sterilized, as you know, before the journey. We wear these oxygen helmets so we can't introduce our bacteria into an ancient atmosphere."

"How do we know which animals to shoot?"

"They're marked with red paint," said Travis. "Today, before our journey, we sent Lesperance here back with the Machine. He came to this particular era and followed certain animals."

"Studying them?"

"Right," said Lesperance. "I track them through their entire existence, noting which of them lives longest. Very few. How many times they mate. Not often. Life's short. When I find one that's going to die when a tree falls on him, or one that drowns in a tar pit, I note the exact hour, minute, and second. I shoot a paint bomb. It leaves a red patch on his hide. We can't miss it. Then I correlate our arrival in the Past so that we meet the Monster not more than two minutes before he would have died anyway. This way, we kill only animals with no future, that are never going to mate again. You see how *careful* we are?"

"But if you came back this morning in Time," said Eckels eagerly, "you must've bumped into *us*, our Safari! How did it turn out? Was it successful? Did all of us get through—alive?"

Travis and Lesperance gave each other a look.

"That'd be a paradox," said the latter. "Time doesn't permit that sort of mess—a man meeting himself. When such occasions threaten, Time steps aside. Like an airplane hitting an air pocket. You felt the Machine jump just before we stopped? That was us passing ourselves on the way back to the Future. We saw nothing. There's no way of telling *if* this expedition was a success, *if* we got our monster, or whether all of us—meaning *you*, Mr. Eckels—got out alive."

Eckels smiled palely.

"Cut that," said Travis sharply. "Everyone on his feet!"

They were ready to leave the Machine.

The jungle was high and the jungle was broad and the jungle was the entire world forever and forever. Sounds like music and sounds like flying tents filled the sky, and those were pterodactyls soaring with cavernous gray wings, gigantic bats out of a delirium and a night fever. Eckels, balanced on the narrow Path, aimed his rifle playfully.

"Stop that!" said Travis. "Don't even aim for fun, damn it! If your gun should go off—"

Eckels flushed. "Where's our *Tyrannosaurus?*"

Lesperance checked his wrist watch. "Up ahead. We'll bisect his trail in sixty seconds. Look for the red paint, for Christ's sake. Don't shoot till we give the word. Stay on the Path. *Stay on the Path!*"

They moved forward in the wind of morning.

"Strange," murmured Eckels. "Up ahead, sixty million years, Election Day over. Keith made President. Everyone celebrating. And here we are, a million years lost, and they don't exist. The things we worried about for months, a lifetime, not even born or thought about yet."

"Safety catches off, everyone!" ordered Travis. "You, first shot, Eckels. Second, Billings. Third, Kramer."

"I've hunted tiger, wild boar, buffalo, elephant, but Jesus, this is *it*," said Eckels. "I'm shaking like a kid."

"Ah," said Travis.

Everyone stopped.

Travis raised his hand. "Ahead," he whispered. "In the mist. There he is. There's His Royal Majesty now."

The jungle was wide and full of twitterings, rustlings, murmurs, and sighs.

Suddenly it all ceased, as if someone had shut a door.

Silence.

A sound of thunder.

Out of the mist, one hundred yards away, came *Tyrannosaurus rex.*

"Jesus God," whispered Eckels.

"Sh!"

It came on great oiled, resilient, striding legs. It towered thirty feet above half of the trees, a great evil god, folding its delicate watchmaker's claws close to its oily reptilian chest. Each lower leg was a piston, a thousand pounds of white bone, sunk in thick ropes of muscle, sheathed over in a gleam of pebbled skin like the mail of a terrible warrior. Each thigh was a ton of meat, ivory, and steel mesh. And from the great breathing cage of the upper body those two delicate arms dangled out front, arms with hands which might pick up and examine men like toys, while the snake neck coiled. And the head itself, a ton of sculptured stone, lifted easily upon the sky. Its mouth gaped, exposing a fence of teeth like daggers. Its eyes rolled, ostrich eggs, empty of all expression save hunger. It closed its mouth in a death grin. It ran, its pelvic bones crushing aside trees and bushes, its taloned feet clawing damp earth, leaving prints six inches deep wherever it settled its weight. It ran with a gliding ballet step, far too poised and balanced for its ten tons. It moved into a sunlit arena warily, its beautifully reptile hands feeling the air.

"My God!" Eckels twitched his mouth. "It could reach up and grab the moon."

"Sh!" Travis jerked angrily. "He hasn't seen us yet."

"It can't be killed." Eckels pronounced this verdict quietly, as if there could be no argument. He had weighed the evidence and this was his considered opinion. The rifle in his hands seemed a cap gun. "We were fools to come. This is impossible."

"Shut up!" hissed Travis.

"Nightmare."

"Turn around," commanded Travis. "Walk quietly to the Machine. We'll remit one half your fee."

"I didn't realize it would be this *big*," said Eckels. "I miscalculated, that's all. And now I want out."

"It *sees* us!"

"There's the red paint on its chest!"

The Thunder Lizard raised itself. Its armored flesh glittered like a thousand green coins. The coins, crusted with slime, steamed.

In the slime, tiny insects wriggled, so that the entire body seemed to twitch and undulate, even while the monster itself did not move. It exhaled. The stink of raw flesh blew down the wilderness.

"Get me out of here," said Eckels. "It was never like this before. I was always sure I'd come through alive. I had good guides, good safaris, and safety. This time, I figured wrong. I've met my match and admit it. This is too much for me to get hold of."

"Don't run," said Lesperance. "Turn around. Hide in the Machine."

"Yes." Eckels seemed to be numb. He looked at his feet as if trying to make them move. He gave a grunt of helplessness.

"Eckels!"

He took a few steps, blinking, shuffling.

"Not *that* way!"

The Monster, at the first motion, lunged forward with a terrible scream. It covered one hundred yards in four seconds. The rifles jerked up and blazed fire. A windstorm from the beast's mouth engulfed them in the stench of slime and old blood. The Monster roared, teeth glittering with sun.

Eckels, not looking back, walked blindly to the edge of the Path, his gun limp in his arms, stepped off the Path, and walked, not knowing it, in the jungle. His feet sank into green moss. His legs moved him, and he felt alone and remote from the events behind.

The rifles cracked again. Their sound was lost in shriek and lizard thunder. The great lever of the reptile's tail swung up, lashed sideways. Trees exploded in clouds of leaf and branch. The Monster twitched its jeweler's hands down to fondle at the men, to twist them in half, to crush them like berries, to cram them into its teeth and its screaming throat. Its boulder-stone eyes leveled with the men. They saw themselves mirrored. They fired at the metallic eyelids and the blazing black iris.

Like a stone idol, like a mountain avalanche, *Tyrannosaurus* fell. Thundering, it clutched trees, pulled them with it. It wrenched and tore the metal Path. The men flung themselves back and away. The body hit, ten tons of cold flesh and stone. The guns fired. The Monster lashed its armored tail, twitched its snake jaws, and lay still. A fount of blood spurted from its throat. Somewhere inside, a sac of fluids burst. Sickening gushes drenched the hunters. They stood, red and glistening.

The thunder faded.

The jungle was silent. After the avalanche, a green peace. After the nightmare, morning.

Billings and Kramer sat on the pathway and threw up. Travis and Lesperance stood with smoking rifles, cursing steadily.

In the Time Machine, on his face, Eckels lay shivering. He had found his way back to the Path, climbed into the Machine.

Travis came walking, glanced at Eckels, took cotton gauze from a metal box, and returned to the others, who were sitting on the Path.

"Clean up."

They wiped the blood from their helmets. They began to curse too. The Monster lay, a hill of solid flesh. Within, you could hear the sighs and murmurs as the furthest chambers of it died, the organs malfunctioning, liquids running a final instant from pocket to sac to spleen, everything shutting off, closing up forever. It was like standing by a wrecked locomotive or a steam shovel at quitting time, all valves being released or levered tight. Bones cracked; the tonnage of its own flesh, off balance, dead weight, snapped the delicate forearms, caught underneath. The meat settled, quivering.

Another cracking sound. Overhead, a gigantic tree branch broke from its heavy mooring, fell. It crashed upon the dead beast with finality.

"There." Lesperance checked his watch. "Right on time. That's the giant tree that was scheduled to fall and kill this animal originally." He glanced at the two hunters. "You want the trophy picture?"

"What?"

"We can't take a trophy back to the Future. The body has to stay right here where it would have died originally, so the insects, birds, and bacteria can get at it, as they were intended to. Everything in balance. The body stays. But we *can* take a picture of you standing near it."

The two men tried to think, but gave up, shaking their heads.

They let themselves be led along the metal Path. They sank wearily into the Machine cushions. They gazed back at the ruined Monster, the stagnating mound, where already strange reptilian birds and golden insects were busy at the steaming armor.

A sound on the floor of the Time Machine stiffened them. Eckels sat there, shivering.

"I'm sorry," he said at last.

"Get up!" cried Travis.

Eckels got up.

"Go out on that Path alone," said Travis. He had his rifle pointed. "You're not coming back in the Machine. We're leaving you here!"

Lesperance seized Travis' arm. "Wait—"

"Stay out of this!" Travis shook his hand away. "This son of a bitch nearly killed us. But it isn't *that* so much. Hell, no. It's his *shoes!* Look at them! He ran off the Path. My God, that *ruins* us! Christ knows how much we'll forfeit! Tens of thousands of dollars of insurance! We guarantee no one leaves the Path. He left it. Oh, the damn fool! I'll have to report to the government. They might revoke our license to travel. God knows *what* he's done to Time, to History!"

"Take it easy, all he did was kick up some dirt."

"How do we *know*?" cried Travis. "We don't know anything! It's all a damn mystery! Get out there, Eckels!"

Eckels fumbled his shirt. "I'll pay anything. A hundred thousand dollars!"

Travis glared at Eckels' checkbook and spat. "Go out there. The Monster's next to the Path. Stick your arms up to your elbows in his mouth. Then you can come back with us."

"That's unreasonable!"

"The Monster's dead, you yellow bastard. The bullets! The bullets can't be left behind. They don't belong in the Past; they might change something. Here's my knife. Dig them out!"

The jungle was alive again, full of the old tremorings and bird cries. Eckels turned slowly to regard that primeval garbage dump, that hill of nightmares and terror. After a long time, like a sleepwalker, he shuffled out along the Path.

He returned, shuddering, five minutes later, his arms soaked and red to the elbows. He held out his hands. Each held a number of steel bullets. Then he fell. He lay where he fell, not moving.

"You didn't have to make him do that," said Lesperance.

"Didn't I? It's too early to tell." Travis nudged the still body. "He'll live. Next time he won't go hunting game like this. Okay." He jerked his thumb wearily at Lesperance. "Switch on. Let's go home."

1492. 1776. 1812.

They cleaned their hands and faces. They changed their caking shirts and pants. Eckels was up and around again, not speaking. Travis glared at him for a full ten minutes.

"Don't look at me," cried Eckels. "I haven't done anything."

"Who can tell?"

"Just ran off the Path, that's all, a little mud on my shoes— what do you want me to do—get down and pray?"

"We might need it. I'm warning you, Eckels, I might kill you yet. I've got my gun ready."

"I'm innocent. I've done nothing!"

1999. 2000. 2055.

The Machine stopped.

"Get out," said Travis.

The room was there as they had left it. But not the same as they had left it. The same man sat behind the same desk. But the same man did not quite sit behind the same desk.

Travis looked around swiftly. "Everything okay here?" he snapped.

"Fine. Welcome home!"

Travis did not relax. He seemed to be looking at the very atoms of the air itself, at the way the sun poured through the one high window.

"Okay, Eckels, get out. Don't ever come back."

Eckels could not move.

"You heard me," said Travis. "What're you *staring* at?"

Eckels stood smelling of the air, and there was a thing to the air, a chemical taint so subtle, so slight, that only a faint cry of his subliminal senses warned him it was there. The colors, white, gray, blue, orange, in the wall, in the furniture, in the sky beyond the window, were . . . were . . . And there was a *feel*. His flesh twitched. His hands twitched. He stood drinking the oddness with the pores of his body. Somewhere, someone must have been screaming one of those whistles that only a dog can hear. His body screamed silence in return. Beyond this room, beyond this wall, beyond this man who was not quite the same man seated at this desk that was not quite the same desk . . . lay an entire world of streets and people. What sort of world it was now, there was no telling. He could feel them moving there, beyond the walls, almost, like so many chess pieces blown in a dry wind. . . .

But the immediate thing was the sign painted on the office wall, the same sign he had read earlier today on first entering.

Somehow, the sign had changed:

TYME SEFARI INC.

SEFARIS TU ANY YEER EN THE PAST.

YU NAIM THE ANIMALL.

WEE TAEK YU THAIR.

YU SHOOT ITT.

Eckels felt himself fall into a chair. He fumbled crazily at the thick slime on his boots. He held up a clod of dirt, trembling. "No, it *can't* be. Not a *little* thing like that. No!"

Embedded in the mud, glistening green and gold and black, was a butterfly, very beautiful, and very dead.

"Not a little thing like *that*! Not a butterfly!" cried Eckels.

It fell to the floor, an exquisite thing, a small thing that could upset balances and knock down a line of small dominoes and then big dominoes and then gigantic dominoes, all down the years across Time. Eckels' mind whirled. It *couldn't* change things. Killing one butterfly couldn't be *that* important! Could it?

His face was cold. His mouth trembled, asking: "Who—who won the presidential election yesterday?"

The man behind the desk laughed. "You joking? You know damn well. Deutscher, of course! Who else? Not that damn weakling Keith. We got an iron man now, a man with guts, by God!" The official stopped. "What's wrong?"

Eckels moaned. He dropped to his knees. He scrabbled at the golden butterfly with shaking fingers. "Can't we," he pleaded to the world, to himself, to the officials, to the Machine, "can't we take it *back*, can't we *make* it alive again? Can't we start over? Can't we—"

He did not move. Eyes shut, he waited, shivering. He heard Travis breathe loud in the room; he heard Travis shift his rifle, click the safety catch, and raise the weapon.

There was a sound of thunder.

RESPONSE

1. Why is Travis so emphatic when he says, "Stay on the Path. Never step off"?

2. Do you agree with Travis when he says, "the cave man . . . is an *entire future nation*"? Explain.

3. Do you think the changes that have taken place by the end of the story can be rightly attributed to Eckels' actions? Give your reasons.

EXTENSION

4. What constructive actions could you take now that would have a long-term benefit for life on this planet?

5. As a class, take action on one environmental issue in your school or community.

On the Loose

Cora A. M. Nelson

> Suggest ways in which flowers could be detrimental to life on earth.

If you've driven past the same marsh on your way to work over the last few summers, you may have observed a growing abundance of tall, purple flowers among the marshland plants. Or perhaps you've noticed an occasional cluster of purple blooms in a roadside ditch, or blanketing the shoreline of a river. If so, you've witnessed another addition to a long list of threats facing Canada's wetlands. The culprit is purple loosestrife (*Lythrum salicaria*).

To many home gardeners, a backdrop of the long-lasting showy blooms offered by lythrum (as all species and varieties of this genus are commonly called) is hard to match. It's a reliable and hardy perennial, flourishing in our northern clime. In a wetland, however, *Lythrum salicaria* can spell disaster.

If water is removed from a shallow wetland to expose the underlying mud, many types of plant seeds that have collected there will sprout; but lythrum seedlings grow quickly and outcompete native varieties in the race for nutrients and light. Each mature plant is capable of producing over 100,000 seeds in its first year. At that rate, it's just a matter of time until lythrum fills the wetland basin with a dense, impenetrable stand, offering virtually no value to man or wildlife.

Native to Eurasia, lythrum seems to have been held in check in its homeland by insect pests. But when the plants crossed the ocean, the insects stayed behind. Its seeds were probably introduced to our shores when the ballast of early settler and cargo ships was dumped into eastern seaboard harbours. Since lythrum was often valued as an herb, some settlers may have intentionally brought seeds with them. They may also have been carried in the wool of sheep, or brought over in unwashed wools which were imported in abundance in the early days of settlement.

Whatever their method of travel, pioneer communities of lythrum soon began to appear all along the east coast and inland along interconnected waterways. It was first recorded in the 1930s as a troublesome weed in floodplain pastures along the St. Lawrence Seaway where it had overtaken and replaced native pasture plants.

Since then, lythrum has spread to many shallow wetlands in the northeastern region of this continent, with pockets appearing across the prairies and west, to the coast. Interestingly, it has been recommended to beekeepers as an excellent choice to "naturalize" along streams as a source of nectar.

To be healthy and productive, a habitat must contain a diversity of plant species. When lythrum becomes established in a shallow wetland, this diversity is forfeited. Cattails and bulrushes are choked out, eliminating nesting sites for waterfowl and material for shelter construction by muskrats. Open water areas grow in and can no longer be used as feeding sites.

Unlike native wetland plants, the tough stalks and branches of lythrum decay slowly, trapping nutrients stored in their tissues instead of releasing them to provide fertile soil for new growth. This low rate of decay also means the wetland basin may fill in with dead plants which block moisture, warmth and light from the soil, inhibiting growth of other plants. The bottom line seems to be that when lythrum moves into a wetland, wildlife and the value of the area as habitat move out.

The challenge of ridding a wetland of unwanted or overgrown plants is a familiar task to biologists and marsh managers. Unfortunately, techniques used in the management of cattails or bulrushes don't work well for lythrum. Removing the water will rid a marsh of dense stands of native emergents, but exposed, damp mud provides just the conditions lythrum seeds require for germination. A manager may unknowingly stimulate a lythrum invasion by managing an area for another plant species.

Mowing doesn't appear to control lythrum either. While seeds are the primary mode of reproduction, lythrum can sprout vegetatively from cuttings of the main stalk. Each slice left behind by mowing may well be the beginning of a new plant. If cutting takes place prior to seed production, enough time may be left for the plants to resprout and set seed within the same growing season. Plants cut later in the year may have already produced seeds, which will sprout in the newly created openings.

Burning, another widely used wetland management technique, has also proved ineffective. In fact, repeated burns seem to stress native plants more than the target species. Lythrum's low ground root stock is protected from fire during the winter, and moisture in the spring and summer limits the burn's intensity. As with mowing, the openings created by fire give seeds already buried in the soil the chance to sprout and grow more vigorously than before.

Extensive flooding of young lythrum seedlings—or co-planting aggressive but favourable wetland plants in areas where lythrum is likely to grow—may offer solutions, but more information on the behaviour of lythrum under these conditions is required.

It's ironic that a plant posing such a threat to wetlands can be promoted as an attractive home garden ornamental. The rationale, however, is that not all of the nursery cultivars have *L. salicaria* in their parentage. Unfortunately, the records conflict in describing the ancestry of some common cultivated varieties.

Records firmly indicate that Morden Pink, a popular strain, was developed as a nearly self-sterile cultivar from *L. virgatum*, a species native to Europe. This variety was then crossed with the native *L. alatum* to develop Morden Rose, Morden Gleam and Columbia Pink. Dropmore Purple is the product of a cross between *L. salicaria* and *L. virgatum*. The cultivars named Happy, Robert, Firecandle, Brightness, The Beacon, Lady Sackville and a few others probably have *L. salicaria* parentage.

In addition to this confusion, researchers are unsure of how each variety responds under different growing conditions. Some think that *L. virgatum* can become invasive, and there is no guarantee that other strains will not become just as problematic. A conscientious home gardener trying to avoid unlabelled cultivars that may be associated with *L. salicaria* will have an impossible task trying to visually tell the varieties apart. And even if a garden is located far from a river or wetland, planted lythrum may still spread. All it takes is for the tiny seeds to wash into a storm sewer, be carried by birds, in the fur of animals, or be blown short distances on the wind, to be transported to just the type of habitat they require.

Too little is known about lythrum in all its varieties. What is certain is that once *L. salicaria* is established in a shallow wetland, the life of that wetland as a healthy, diverse ecosystem comes to an end. If you find lythrum growing in your area, inform a local conservation authority. If you already have it in your garden, consider replacing it. Dig it out, being careful to take all of the root, and put it with the garbage for proper disposal. Choose alternatives for planting such as Blazing Star, Morden Beauty, or Coral Bell. That way, you can enjoy the same showy displays in your back yard without contributing to the potential destruction of our fragile wetland environment.

RESPONSE

1. Discuss the properties of lythrum that make it a threat to wetlands.

2. Discuss the ways in which wetland managers could deal with lythrum.

EXTENSION

3. To what extent should human beings intervene in natural processes? Provide specific examples to support your opinion.

4. Write a report that examines the way in which your community manages plant life.

Antaeus in Manhattan

Lewis Thomas

In what ways do you think insect populations are similar to human populations?

Insects again.

When social animals are gathered together in groups, they become qualitatively different creatures from what they were when alone or in pairs. Single locusts are quiet, meditative, sessile things, but when locusts are added to other locusts, they become excited, change color, undergo spectacular endocrine revisions, and intensify their activity until, when there are enough of them packed shoulder to shoulder, they vibrate and hum with the energy of a jet airliner and take off.

Watson, Nel, and Hewitt have collected large numbers of termites in the field and placed them together for observation, in groups and pairs. The grouped termites become increasingly friendly and active, but show no inclination to lay eggs or mate; instead, they cut down on their water intake, watching their weight, and the mitochondria of their flight muscles escalate in metabolic activity. Grouped termites keep touching each other incessantly with their antennae, and this appears to be the central governing mechanism. It is the being touched that counts, rather than the act of touching. Deprived of antennae, any termite can become a group termite if touched frequently enough by the others.

Isolated, paired termites are something else again. As soon as they are removed from the group, and the touching from all sides comes to an end, they become aggressive, standoffish; they begin drinking compulsively, and abstain from touching each other. Sometimes, they even bite off the distal halves of each other's antennae, to eliminate the temptation. Irritably, settling down to make the best of a poor situation, they begin preparations for the laying of eggs and the taking care of the brood. Meanwhile, the mitochondria in their flight muscles go out of business.

The most intensely social animals can only adapt to group behavior. Bees and ants have no option when isolated, except to die. There is really no such creature as a single individual; he has no more life of his own than a cast-off cell marooned from the surface of your skin.

Ants are more like the parts of an animal than entities on their own. They are mobile cells, circulating through a dense connective tissue of other ants in a matrix of twigs. The circuits are so intimately woven that the anthill meets all the essential criteria of an organism.

It would be wonderful to understand how the anthill communication system works. Somehow, by touching each other continually, by exchanging bits of white stuff carried about in their mandibles like money, they manage to inform the whole enterprise about the state of the world outside, the location of food, the nearness of enemies, the maintenance requirements of the Hill, even the direction of the sun; in the Alps, mountaineers are said to use the ameboid configurations of elongated ant nests as pointers to the south. The Hill, for its part, responds by administering the affairs of the institution, coordinating and synchronizing the movements of its crawling parts, aerating and cleaning the nest so that it can last for as long as forty years, fetching food in by long tentacles, rearing broods, taking slaves, raising crops, and, at one time or another, budding off subcolonies in the near vicinity, as progeny.

The social insects, especially ants, have been sources of all kinds of parables, giving lessons in industry, interdependence, altruism, humility, frugality, patience. They have been employed to instruct us in the whole range of our institutional virtues, from the White House to your neighborhood savings bank.

And now, at last, they have become an Art Form. A gallery in New York exhibited a collection of 2 million live army ants, on loan from Central America, in a one-colony show entitled "Patterns and Structures." They were displayed on sand in a huge square bin, walled by plastic sides high enough to prevent them from crawling over and out into Manhattan. The inventor of the work arranged and rearranged the location of food sources in different places, according to his inspiration and their taste, and they formed themselves into long, black, ropy patterns, extended like writhing limbs, hands, fingers, across the sand in crescents, crisscrosses, and long ellipses, from one station to another. Thus deployed, they were watched with intensity by the crowds of winter-carapaced people who lined up in neat rows to gaze down at them. The ants were, together with the New Yorkers, an abstraction, a live mobile, an action painting, a piece of found art, a happening, a parody, depending on the light.

I can imagine the people moving around the edges of the plastic barrier, touching shoulder to shoulder, sometimes touching hands, exchanging bits of information, nodding, smiling sometimes, prepared as New Yorkers always are to take flight at a moment's notice, their mitochondria fully stoked and steaming. They move in orderly lines around the box, crowding one another precisely, without injury, peering down, nodding, and then backing off to let new people in. Seen from a distance, clustered densely around the white plastic box containing the long serpentine lines of army ants, turning to each other and murmuring repetitively, they seem an absolute marvel. They might have dropped here from another planet.

I am sad that I did not see any of this myself. By the time I had received the communication on television and in my morning paper, felt the tugging pull toward Manhattan, and made my preparations to migrate, I learned that the army ants had all died.

The Art Form simply disintegrated, all at once, like one of those exploding, vanishing faces in paintings by the British artist Francis Bacon.

There was no explanation, beyond the rumored, unproved possibility of cold drafts in the gallery over the weekend. Monday morning they were sluggish, moving with less precision, dully. Then, the death began, affecting first one part and then another, and within a day all 2 million were dead, swept away into large plastic bags and put outside for engulfment and digestion by the sanitation truck.

It is a melancholy parable. I am unsure of the meaning, but I do think it has something to do with all that plastic—that, and the distance from the earth. It is a long, long way from the earth of a Central American jungle to the ground floor of a gallery, especially when you consider that Manhattan itself is suspended on a kind of concrete platform, propped up by a meshwork of wires, pipes, and water mains. But I think it was chiefly the plastic, which seems to me the most unearthly of all man's creations so far. I do not believe you can suspend army ants away from the earth, on plastic, for any length of time. They will lose touch, run out of energy, and die for lack of current.

One steps on ants, single ants or small clusters, every day without giving it a thought, but it is impossible to contemplate the death of so vast a beast as these 2 million ants without feeling twinges of sympathy, and something else. Nervously, thinking this way, thinking especially about Manhattan and the plastic platform, I laid down my newspaper and reached for the book on my shelf that contained, I knew, precisely the paragraph of reassurance required by the moment:

It is not surprising that many analogies have been drawn between the social insects and human societies. Fundamentally, however, these are misleading or meaningless, for the behavior of insects is rigidly stereotyped and determined by innate instructive mechanisms; they show little or no insight or capacity for learning, and they lack the ability to develop a social tradition based on the accumulated experience of many generations.

It is, of course, an incomplete comfort to read this sort of thing to one's self. For full effect, it needs reading aloud by several people at once, moving the lips in synchrony.

RESPONSE

1. How do insects appear to communicate with each other?
2. "Bees and ants have no option when isolated, except to die."
   a) Explain why this phenomenon occurs among bees and ants.
   b) Do you think there is a correlation between isolation and death among human beings as well? Explain.
3. What was the purpose of the "Patterns and Structures" exhibition?
4. Explain the ways in which the behaviour of the ants and the behaviour of the spectators at the exhibit were similar.

EXTENSION

5. "It is a melancholy parable. I am unsure of the meaning. . . ." With a partner or in a small group, interpret the meaning of this "melancholy parable."
6. Investigate the myth of Antaeus. How is the myth related to Thomas' essay?
7. For discussion: Is there any kind of relationship between humans and insects?

A Guide's Guide to Technology

David Harms

What is technology? What are the purposes of technology? Illustrate your answer with specific examples.

It was a hot, windless July afternoon, and the only motion of the boat came from our shifting bodies, sending small ripples out over the glass. I dropped my jig some sixty-five feet to the lake bottom (like most guides, I violate the letter of the law and fish with my guests) and began a slow undulating retrieve. Ten feet up one of Waterbury's innumerable five pound lake trout took the lure, and seconds later another bent Alan's rod tip to the water. Vern remained fishless in the bow. He took his pipe out of his mouth and tapped the bowl empty on the gunwale. "What I don't get," he said, "is why you guides don't use depth finders. Make the fishin' a hell of a lot better."

Waterbury Lake lies 120 miles south of the NWT/Saskatchewan border. As in the heavily populated south, the number of electronic fish-locating devices in evidence is inversely proportional to the number of fish, with the difference that the latter, and not the former, abound. In the quarter century since the lodge opened, the technological component of the day's sport has changed little. Guests still fish with no more assistance than that offered by a motorboat, their own tackle, and the guide's knowledge.

As one of those guides I was at first enchanted by the prospect of using a graph or flasher (two variations of depth finder which can indicate fish as well as water depth) to explore unfished areas of the lake and zero in on trophy holding holes. On reflection, I have found this issue to be more complex. There is no question that under most circumstances fish-locating devices can help an intelligent fisherman catch more fish, and that in itself isn't a bad thing. My concern is with the way the use of this technology changes the character of the fishing experience.

Witness my guests, Alan and Vern, in their other incarnation as modern day Great Lakes fishermen. Alan is comfortably seated at the helm of an 18 foot fiberglass boat, a ninety horsepower outboard hanging off the stern and sputtering along at trolling speed. On slowly scrolling paper, a graph recorder sketches out the world below. Between a thick, level line describing the surface, and another irregular one for the bottom, there appears a scattered array of arches, each one a fish of several pounds or more. Alan touches a series of keypads on the graph and its scale changes so it now only displays the water between 85 feet and the lake bed at 100 feet. The bottom separates into an uneven baseline and a tight maze of arches, lake trout hugging the rocks.

"Drop the flutter spoon to 95," he calls to his partner. Vern steps to the starboard rod. Like the other three rods it is paired to a downrigger, a winch with a short arm which lowers a seven and a half pound lead ball into the water. The fishing line is attached to the ball by a quick-release device which frees the line and lure from the heavy weight when a fish strikes, enabling the fisherman to play his catch unencumbered. Vern's fingers play over the downrigger's control panel. As the electric motor pays out the cable, he feeds line from the reel. This done, he snugs the line, bending the rod into a tight half circle. He enters a series of keystrokes on the control panel of the next downrigger, and in obedience to its little electronic mind it begins alternately raising and lowering the line a few feet at a time in a hopefully attractive manner. Suddenly, one of the rods pops straight, then begins to bob crazily.

"Mine!" yells Alan, "take the wheel!" He pumps the rod and reels furiously, fairly rocketing the hapless seven pound brown trout from the depths. The fish surfaces twenty feet behind the still moving boat, bloated by its rapid ascent. Alan skis it along the wake and into the net. "Beaut," says Vern. "Yeah, and not a bad fighter for his size." The fish is killed and put into the cooler, from where it will eventually find its way to the compost heap after Alan's wife again refuses to clean his catch.

By the end of the day the men have succeeded in boating a number of trout and salmon, with several of the latter weighing over twenty pounds. They are two proud, happy guys with a hefty legal limit of fish, but what is it they have been doing all day? Fishing??

Neither man has had physical contact with the device traditionally employed in sport fishing (that is, the assembly of rod, reel, line and lure) for more than an hour. Instead, they have demonstrated their dedication to the sport by scrutinizing the graph printout and temperature probe display, constantly reprogramming the downriggers for maximum effect, and filtering the ongoing CB chatter for information on the best lure choices for the day. They have become highly efficient fish catching machines, but in this narrowing of focus they have lost the greater value of the experience of fishing.

Think of another fisherman. He is all of twelve years old, and he is adventuring along a western stream folded into a small valley. He carries a stick and a tiny hook tied to it with a length of pirated monofilament. Beside a shallow riffle he stoops and picks a small conical form from a submerged rock. He breaks it open, extracts its creator—a black headed, olive bodied caddisfly larva with spindly, grasping legs—and baits his hook with it.

He walks a few feet down a gravel bar left by the spring freshet, and at its terminus he swings his bait out over a deep pool. As it hits the surface a four inch rainbow trout darts up and engulfs it, and a split second later is high in the air, wet and wriggling. The boy releases the fish, jumps a narrow backwater to the streambank and continues downstream. The stream splits around an island; just before the lesser flow rejoins the greater, it forms a small waterfall over an old log. Below the log is a small pool, still and impenetrable. Sunlight flickers through the leaves, lines of bubbles and dust circle lazily on the pool's surface. The boy knows this is the place—it has that colour, sound, feel and smell to it. He procures another caddis. His pulse quickens. Now he is not a fisherman, but a conjurer, exercising his art and calling on benevolent spirits to coax the leviathan from its lair.

On his first two efforts the bait falls short, and he pulls it from the water before the small fish can rob the hook. The third time it falls next to the bank, just below the waterfall. It sinks into the blackness. The boy watches the line where it pierces the pool's surface, like a thin blade of grass. Did it move? He waits. The line twitches, he lifts the stick and feels an incredible weight. In his eagerness to see the fish and his fear of losing it he runs straight back and pulls it up onto the gravel, a glorious, brilliantly coloured, fat bellied, eight inch rainbow trout.

It has swallowed the hook deeply. Solemnly he takes out a rusty pocketknife and clips the line. He returns the fish to the stream, where time and the creature's digestive juices will dissolve the metal. The boy has no more means to fish that day, but he also has no more need to fish. He turns up the path, already rehearsing his tale.

This story has something in common with the preceding story. The boy (and I think I can speak on his behalf, having once been him) was hoping, like Alan and Vern, to catch that one monster fish. It differs from the first tale in its plurality. Fishing, in the boy's experience, is not just catching fish. It is locating a suitable branch for a rod, knowing where to find the caddis larvae that the trout love, and knowing also that a shirt pocket full of caddis can liberate themselves by crawling up the fabric if one is inattentive. It is the coolness of the forest in summer and the changing song of the stream as it seeks out the ocean. It is far more than putting a hook in a trout's mouth.

Alan and Vern's loss is becoming more apparent. They have focused on numbers and size of fish caught, ignoring all else. If fishing at its best is a complex whole, like a good story, then they have discarded all but a paragraph and set the remainder in garishly bold type. Time spent getting to know a body of water and the habits of its residents is replaced by time on the job, earning the means to purchase instant electronic proficiency.

The device has supplanted their engagement, or relatedness with the world, and in so doing it has equated the depth of the fishing experience with the relative shallowness of the commodity—fish.

It is one thing to deplore the bastardizing effect of a certain technology on a traditional pursuit, and another to know how to respond. Albert Borgmann offers a direction, pointing out that "if we recognize the central vacuity of advanced technology, that emptiness can become the opening for focal things."* What, in this case, does the realization open to?

The experience of the boy can be a starting point. He is not a weekend fisherman on the stream's banks for the first time, he is one of its familiars. The barriers that say I am I and not You and not this Tree have not yet come to him, and when the high water

*Albert Borgmann, *Technology and the Character of Contemporary Life* (Chicago: University of Chicago Press, 1984), p. 199.

of spring sweeps away last year's trout refuge he feels the loss, and must rebuild himself in some small way as the stream rebuilds itself. He knows what most adults are acculturated against knowing, that his skin is not the boundary of his self. His focal experience is a unity of mind and body, of body and world. As such it is not coldly rational and efficient, though it may have rational and efficient characteristics, but sensual, visceral and poetic.

Such a focal experience of fishing has profound implications for the profession of guiding. At Waterbury, the obstacles to a centred approach are less than they might be. Certainly, the idyllic streamside metaphor is somewhat diminished by the use of power boats; islands and points have a tendency to blur when sped past, and the lake itself from those who move too quickly over it. Still, with the exception of spring and fall when the lake trout are in shallow water and guests are not easily dissuaded from trolling, most fish are caught by jigging and casting, activities which require a form of unity of mind, body and environment, and which permit the boat to be anchored, drifted silently, or dispensed with altogether. It is a simple, uncluttered approach, and it rests heavily on the guide's knowledge rather than on the calculated benevolence of a silicon webwork.

This should be preserved and enhanced. The guide has an entire summer (perhaps many summers) on the lake and is potential heir to deep knowledge about it. If all he does is procure fish for his guests, then he will in time be replaced by a device, in the interests of economy, but if he makes of his fishing and guiding a focal practice, he opens up a vast world for himself and his guests.

A focal practice is rich in context and nuance, and so is not strictly quantifiable. General guidelines for a focal practice of fishing may, however, be suggested.

This practice resists the narrow, technologized view of fishing as the acquisition of increasing numbers and sizes of fish. It grasps the physical, mental, emotional and spiritual context of the experience. It recognizes the connectedness of things. It knows that technology must be the servant of meaningfulness, not its milieu. A fish is not something only to be caught, but also nurtured, revered, eaten (in full flavour and with thanks) set free, and meditated on.

In writing this I am faced with a dilemma. I have stated my argument in such a way that quality and quantity are frequently diametrically opposed. The former becomes the province of eloquence (optima), the latter the domain of efficiency (maxima), and in that arrangement I am unmistakably on the side of quality. My problem is that I do not perceive that quality makes any sense when held to the light of quantity, or vice versa. Fishing as the availability of a technologically produced commodity has no truck with fishing as a merging of the individual with nature. Is the choice between the two purely arbitrary?

My gut feeling, or my unconscious, or my soul, if you will, tells me that life is more like a story than an equation. Most of us, at one time or another, in our childhood if at all, have felt wonderment at life. We have seen the story unfolding in its complexity and beauty, and within it maxima has its place. It is only when we exalt it at the expense of the story that we do violence to life.

RESPONSE

1. Do you agree that although Alan and Vern have become highly efficient at catching fish, they have lost the greater value of the experience of fishing? Defend your point of view.

2. How has the author used the story of the boy to show that "technology must be the servant of meaningfulness"?

3. Explain the author's dilemma as recounted at the end of the essay.

EXTENSION

4. In a small group, explore the ways in which technology has invaded other sports and pastimes.

5. Develop a set of criteria to determine the appropriateness of any new technology.

Human Behaviour

Humour

Morals and Ethics

Relationships

Science and Technology

Essays

Articles

Editorials

Debate

Remembrance

Short Stories

Memoir

English Tale

A U T H O R   I N D E X

p. 3: From ALL I REALLY NEED TO KNOW I LEARNED IN KINDERGARTEN by Robert Fulghum. Reprinted with the permission of Villard Books, a division of Random House, Inc.; **p. 6**: "Eliciting Human Potential" from THE BEST OF SYDNEY J. HARRIS by Sydney J. Harris. Copyright © 1975, 1976, 1978, 1979, 1980, 1981 by the Chicago Daily News, The Chicago Sun-Times, Field Newspaper Syndicate, and Sydney J. Harris. Copyright © 1982 by Sydney J. Harris. Reprinted by permission of Houghton Mifflin Company; **p. 8**: Reprinted from ESQUIRE, August 1986, by permission; **p. 13**: Copyright, 1988, U.S. News & World Report; **p. 16**: Reprinted by permission of Joan L. Ullyot, M.D.; **p. 20**: Reprinted from CANADIAN DIMENSION, October 1987, by permission; **p. 23**: Reprinted from CHATELAINE, May 1988, by permission of Dr. Calvin Stiller and Dr. D. Alan Shewmon; **p. 28**: Reprinted from Ms. Magazine, October 1987, by permission of Suzanne P. Harwood, M.D.; **p. 32**: Reprinted with permission of Atheneum Publishers, an imprint of Macmillan Publishing Company from AMERICAN BEAT by Bob Greene. Copyright © 1983 John Deadline Enterprises; **p. 39**: "Margaret Laurence: A Remembrance for CBC's Morningside" by Timothy Findley. Copyright © 1987, Pebble Productions Inc. Appeared in *Grail*, December 1987; **p. 42**: From THE SNOW WALKER by Farley Mowat. Reprinted by permission of the author; **p. 51**: From ALL I REALLY NEED TO KNOW I LEARNED IN KINDERGARTEN by Robert Fulghum. Reprinted with the permission of Villard Books, a division of Random House, Inc.; **p. 53**: Copyright © 1988 Margaret Visser. Reprinted by permission of the author; **p. 56**: Copyright © Garrison Keillor, 1987. Reprinted by permission of Penguin Books Canada Limited; **p. 63**: "Mister Blink" by Michel Tremblay, c/o John C. Goodwin & Associates, 839 Sherbrooke est, Suite 2, Montréal, Québec, H2L 1K6. Translated by Michael Bullock who is Professor Emeritus of Creative Writing at the University of British Columbia. Reprinted by permission; **p. 66**: Reprinted by permission of Don Congdon Associates, Inc. Copyright © 1953, renewed 1981 by Ray Bradbury; **p. 71**: "Trade the World Debt Crisis for Ecological Preservation" reprinted by permission of Tom Falvey; **p. 75**: An excerpt from END THE ARMS RACE: FUND HUMAN NEEDS, edited by Dr. Thomas L. Perry and Dr. James G. Foulks. Reprinted by kind permission of Gordon Soules Book Publishers Ltd.; **p. 85**: Reprinted from DISCOVER Magazine, July 1987, by permission of Russell L. Schweickart; **p. 91**: "Canadians: What Do They Want?" by Margaret Atwood, from MOTHER JONES, January 1982. Reprinted by permission; **p. 99**: "God Is Not a Fish Inspector" by W. D. Valgardson is reprinted from *God Is Not a Fish Inspector* by permission of Oberon Press; **p. 111**: Reprinted with permission of Canada and the World magazine, Oakville, Ontario; **p. 116**: From *The Thrill of the Grass* by W. P. Kinsella. Copyright © W. P. Kinsella, 1984. Reprinted by permission of Penguin Books Canada Limited; **p. 125**: Reprinted with permission of Canada and the World magazine, Oakville, Ontario; **p. 130**: Copyright © 1963 by Peter Beagle. First published in *The Atlantic Monthly*. Reprinted by permission of McIntosh and Otis, Inc.; **p. 149**: From MAY YOUR FIRST LOVE BE YOUR LAST by Gregory Clark. Used by permission of the Canadian Publishers, McClelland and Stewart, Toronto, and by permission of Estate of Gregory Clark; **p. 154**: Reprinted with permission Ms. Magazine, Copyright 1988; **p. 158**: From THE MAID OF THE NORTH: FEMINIST FOLK TALES FROM AROUND THE WORLD. Copyright © 1981 by Ethel Johnston Phelps. Reprinted by permission of Henry Holt and Company, Inc.; **p. 165**: Reprinted with permission Ms. Magazine, Copyright 1988; **p. 169**: REPRINTED WITH PERMISSION FROM PSYCHOLOGY TODAY MAGAZINE Copyright © 1988 (PT Partners, L.P.); **p. 175**: Reprinted from Science Dimension, National Research Council of Canada. The opinions expressed by Fernand Seguin are his own, and are not to be confused with policy statements of Science Dimension's publisher, the National Research Council of Canada; **p. 179**: Copyright © 1957 by Loren Eiseley. Reprinted from THE IMMENSE JOURNEY by Loren